casanova

by SUSPECT CULTURE

cast in alphabetical order

Mabel Aitken	Mrs Tennant
Paul Blair	Casanova
Callum Cuthbertson	Cabinet Maker
Vicki Liddelle	Kate
Louise Ludgate	Marie Louise

Direction + design	Graham Eatough
Text	David Greig
Music	Nick Powell
Lighting design	Ian Scott
Company manager	Shona Rattray
Technical manager	Nicky Rintoul
Graphic design + design consultant	Patrick Macklin
Costume design	Pamela Carter
Assistant stage managers	Kay Hesford, Sam Martin

Original music recorded by Nick Powell with additional instrumentation from
Alex Lee (guitar, keyboards), Lucy Wilkins (violin) and Sarah Wilson (cello)

Casanova is produced in association with the Tron Theatre, Glasgow

Vicki Liddelle as 'Kate' and Gavin Mitchell as 'Casanova' at the Tron Theatre, February 2001

My interest in Casanova as a potential Suspect Culture project began in 1998 with the company's first annual symposium entitled Theatre and the Sciences of the Mind. An attempt to find connections between the two different spheres, the day consisted of workshops, seminars and lectures that explored ideas of mutual interest to both disciplines. In a lecture about the formation of character, one of the speakers referred to Casanova as an example of a 'real' person who had invented different characters for himself throughout his life. He would 'perform' these characters in order to ingratiate himself into whichever European court he was visiting at the time. Casanova's fictitious creations usually succeeded in either extracting money from or sleeping with the various courtiers he encountered. This self-conscious presentation of character seemed to connect with ideas the company was interested in exploring at the time and the issues raised by Casanova's lifestyle an interesting starting point for a new show.

Even a reasonably superficial look at the copious twelve volumes of memoirs Casanova produced towards the end of his life leads the reader to a couple of interesting conclusions. Firstly, even allowing for all the usual embellishments of autobiography, his life was a very glamorous, trans-European adventure. Secondly, according to the author, there was a very different attitude behind Casanova's relationships with women (and interestingly in a couple of instances, men) than a modern view of a casanova figure might suggest. Casanova presents his promiscuity as part of a coherent philosophical position, which involves the celebration of pleasure and life lived for the moment. However, this is not simply a selfish pursuit of pleasure and Casanova claims to be as interested in his partners' happiness as his own.

Both these elements of glamour and moral complexity were important ingredients in a contemporary sphere for our modern Casanova. The international art scene, albeit in an exaggerated form, seemed to me an appropriate context for some of the ideas suggested by the memoirs, and the gallery an interesting setting for seduction.

The project went through two key workshop phases. The first was in Prague with a group of Czech performers during Suspect Culture's Mainstream tour of 2000 and the second was in Glasgow with a group of nine female performers later in the same year. Both workshops explored different seduction strategies and the different levels of complicity involved with these seductions. The Prague workshop was particularly interesting because the city has many connections with the original Casanova. There is a story that he was in Prague around the time of the premiere of Mozart's opera Don Giovanni and even helped Da Ponte the librettist finish a couple of scenes. These coincidences have also found their way into the piece and Don Giovanni is as important an influence on the structure of our piece as anything in the memoirs. A personal interest in operatic styles in general has also influenced the ways in which the different moral positions contained within the piece are presented I think.

Between the first performances in Spring 2001 and the subsequent run at the Edinburgh Festival significant changes were made in an attempt to refine our ideas and their presentation. As with any Suspect Culture show it has been this slow process of influence and coincidence, individual preferences and collaboration that has resulted in what you will see tonight. All these factors have combined into a modern Casanova in a very rich historical and literary tradition.

Graham Eatough

Men, Women and Casanovas

Casanova: the eponym for a sexually successful man.

That's the definition given in Cassell's Dictionary of Slang. And term for a sexually successful woman? Littered as it is with tragic whores, femme fatales and absurd nymphomaniacs, our cultural history just doesn't seem to provide an adequate female equivalent. No term, and certainly no eponym, conveys the notion of success without shame or carries with it the glory of a life lived in the pursuit of pleasure quite like 'Casanova' does.

The theories and arguments, demonstrated and expounded as to why this might be, as to what oppressions this perpetrates, as to how this should (or should not) be redressed, are many. And they'll remain in constant revision and circulation as long as gender remains an 'issue.'

But perhaps Casanova can be made useful both sides of the biological divide by looking a little more closely at what our legendary hero was really all about.

It is worth adding a few more details to the somewhat sketchy figure who went by the name of Giacomo Casanova. By all accounts (which are, on the whole, his accounts) he was a man of letters, an entrepreneur, a spy, a soldier, and, of course, a prolific and accomplished lover, who cut a dash in the courts and salons of eighteenth century Europe. He might also be described as having been a thief, a liar, a petty swindler, a cheat, a jailbird, and, by today's standards, an incestuous paedophile. Sensual, clever and charming he may have been, however, we might also reasonably think of him of having been vain, self-important, delusional, covetous, humourless (specifically where he himself is concerned), ridiculous, sexually incontinent, and utterly, almost animally, amoral.

This is all by the by though because pop-culture Casanova is remembered for sex and sex alone - which is wholly appropriate - but it's not the kind of sex the original was engaged in. Mis-remembered as the arch-seducer, the timeless legend of Casanova still sashays about the piano bar of our collective imagination working his way into and out of the beds of poor foolish woman after poor foolish woman: their romantic hopes raised only ever to be dashed because their dreamy desires

Photography by Pamela Carter

Prague Casanova workshop, Archa Theatre May 2000

will never match those of the rampant lover. So what is it that [these] women want? It's a recurring question if only banally posed by the film industry, self-help manuals or glossy magazines. But is it even worth asking? The Viennese gentleman who first wondered, worried, and wondered some more to unwittingly produce a whole century of sexual inadequacies posed his question perhaps because, in the game of comparing his and hers, he found that her desire didn't stand to attention and salute quite like his did.

Sexual difference has become sexual anxiety since Casanova but it was never so for him neither the women who enjoyed his company. Stefan Zweig, in an often scathing assessment of Casanova's life and work, grants him genius precisely because he was not a seducer. He didn't trick, manipulate or coerce women into having sex with him; the only thing he insisted upon was that they gave themselves freely. 'What do women want?' was a spurious question for Casanova because they wanted exactly as he did: pleasure for pleasure's sake. He was, Zweig writes, 'an altruist in love.'

His genius was then his absolute abandonment to, his courageous commitment to the adventure of sexual pleasure: for men and women both. And, be honest, you can't get much fairer than that, can you? If we think of Casanova less as a prowling sex pest and more as the embodiment of honest-to-goodness bared-faced pleasure then we might, however momentarily, be able to set aside the issue of gender just long enough to enjoy ourselves.

But one thing does continue to bother me, and maybe I should consider it my problem and no-one else's, and it's that I still can't happily answer the question I have often asked myself since we began making **Casanova**. Why, in 2001, can't I imagine a female Casanova on stage without getting anxious?

Pamela Carter

Some Casanova reading:
L'Histoire de ma Vie, Giacomo Casanova
Casanova: A study in self-portraiture, Stefan Zweig
Casanova: Or the art of happiness, Lydia Flem

Dana Poláková in the Prague 'Casanova' workshop

Photography by Pamela Carter

The Rules of Seduction

It surprised me that I felt aggressive towards him. I'd never met the man before. We had barely begun to speak. Yet I wanted to kick his face in. He was sitting opposite me on a red leather armchair in an Edinburgh pub. I can't reveal his real name, for obvious reasons, but it's fair to say he was, and still is Scotland's Casanova. He is reputed to have slept with well over a thousand women. His existence had been unknown to me until, on hearing about Suspect Culture's Casanova Project, a woman friend suggested I talk to him. 'For research,' she said. 'You never know,' she said, 'he might give you some ideas.'

At the time I'd ignored it. I've always believed that the writer's job is to imagine himself into the character. Observation is for sociologists. Besides, I thought, I can always draw on my own experience. I'm not irresistible to women, of course, but - I do OK, I do just fine. There must be in me, somewhere in my psyche, a Casanova. In all men, surely? To write him is just a matter of... getting in touch with my inner lothario.

So I worked for a few months on a script and got nowhere. It's not easy writing chat up lines destined to be spoken by a man labelled 'the world's greatest lover'. I may as well have been a monkey at the typewriter. I was producing screeds of material but none of it rang true. None of it was, in fact, seductive. Which is why, against all my instincts, I finally found myself dialling his number and arranging to meet.

It was Valentine's day. The February air hung half frozen in front of a low sun. The heat from shoppers' lungs condensed into wet clouds and steamed the windows of the card shops. It was that day of the year when dangerous un-nameable desires are made safe. The day when the alchemy of a greetings card turns base lust, need, and longing into the gold-leaf kitsch of love.

I asked him if he'd sent a Valentine. 'No,' he said. 'Received any?' 'A few,' he replied, 'Yeah, a few'. He reached into the pocket of his black leather jacket and drew out a small white card. He slid it across the table to me. I opened it and read. The red light of the pub fire played across the words. 'Roses are red. Violets are blue. I want to fuck and be fucked by - you.' I looked at him. His face was poker straight. 'Do you know who sent it?' I asked. He nodded his head towards the slim, dark haired young woman who was washing pint glasses behind the bar. She noticed him looking and caught his eye; a half smile lit her face before she returned to her work. It was at that moment that the sudden tug of aggression in my gut took me by surprise. I passed the card back to him.

I had fancied her. When I walked into the bar she had caught my eye. I had made a special effort to be pleasant as I ordered the drinks. And all the time, behind my back, she was lusting after – after this specimen, this skinny, bespectacled piece of cocksure slag in front of me. 'Do you have any idea what you're getting herself into?' I wanted to yell at her. 'I – me – I could be good for you. But him – this – never.' The emotion boiled and died in an instant like milk in a pan. But its violence interested me. It was illuminating. The man I was talking to makes men angry. He makes them feel as though they're about to be stolen from.

DG   Before I came here today, the reason I was interested in you was because I expected you to be followed around by legions of angry women. When in fact, so far as I can tell, the women you've been with remain... friendly.

C   Steady.

DG   Well, you know... when they talk about you they're not aggressive. They're... sarcastic sometimes but in the end, if anything, it seems they adopt a wistful tone.

C   I wouldn't know.

DG   You're not curious? About how you're talked about, behind your back?

C   No. I'm interested in what people say to my

face. I think people tell the truth when they talk to you one on one. When they talk in groups they say what they think people want to hear.

DG   Do you get a lot of aggression from men?

C   Yeah.

DG   What sort of thing? Violence?

C   Rarely. More often it's a kind of low grade contempt whenever I'm in male company. I get taken aside quite a lot. Told that if I go near his friend, his sister, his daughter etc that he'll kill me. There's a lot of moralising from men. These are guys who who've all indulged in some pathetic adultery or other, maybe they even go to prostitutes – but, you know, I'm beyond the pale. I'm sick.

DG   Does that surprise you?

C   No. The truth of the matter is, most men don't like women. They're not very interested in them. Whenever they can, straight men seek out the company of other men. If you like women you're seen as being a bit queer. A bit sissy. As far as most men are concerned, a woman ceases to exist the moment she's out of his sight. Men hate me because I remind them that the women in their lives have their own desires, their own existence. I'm the wolf outside the cottage door. Except of course, I'm not. The wolf is the woman herself.

Suddenly his phone went off. He apologised and checked who was calling him. 'Do you mind if I take this call?' he asked. 'It's important.' I nodded. He took out a folded sheet of paper from his jacket pocket.

'The rules you asked for. I typed them up last night.' He pushed the paper towards me and then wandered towards the back of the pub where he could talk to... whoever it was.

I couldn't help trying to imagine who was calling him. I saw some London executive, up in Edinburgh for a meeting with the suits at Scottish Widows or wherever. She's suddenly bored with the talk about interest rates and rugby matches and she sneaks out to call Casanova. Later I told him the picture I had conjured and he said it was essentially true except that she ran a fish farm and had come down from Orkney. They'd met on millennium night when he happened to be up in Kirkwall. Amongst the fireworks, they'd shared a night he described, maddeningly, as 'transcendental', and the next morning they went their separate ways into the year 2000. I wanted to hit him again. What was it? Fear? Did I envy him? Did I despise him?

I looked at the rules of seduction. I'd asked him, as a research tool, to give me a list of techniques. He was sexually successful on a grand scale. How did he do it? The list, I think it's fair to say, took me aback. The

force of what he'd written, the sheer... baldness of the analysis. I suppose I had expected hints and tips - instead he'd given me something almost like a philosophy, a way of living. How can a man achieve such... distance in the face of such intimate experiences.

DG I've looked at this and...I'm a bit shocked.

C You asked for it.

DG No, I asked...I mean, it's brilliant material for the project but, as a human being it shocks me... that you can be... what's the word...?

C Detached.

DG Yeah. Detached. That you can be detached enough to...

C I've been thinking about it a lot recently. It's been on my mind.

DG So... this... you've been working on it?

C I've been looking at things. Trying to understand them. I - I'll be honest with you - I'm not sure I'm able to be the kind of person I am, anymore. It's tiring. It's feels like I'm a fucking spy or something, and I have no - you know - no public life. I believe in it, I believe in what I do but I'm out on my own. I'm in the cold. I want to stop.

DG You're concerned about the morality of sleeping with hundreds of women?

C No. I'm concerned about the weight of responsibility. Married couples need me to exist so that they can remain married. The woman dreams of me, the man dreams of being married. That way they don't tear each other apart. But in fact - I spend most of my time alone. I'm alone. I'll have to stop sometime. Perhaps that sometime is coming soon.

DG You think you might meet the right woman?

C I might.

His eyes were cast down towards his distorted reflection in the black mahogany of the table. It was as though he was peering down into it's darkness hoping to catch a glimpse of her. But maybe I read too much into things. He was probably just tired. He was probably just shy of meeting my gaze.

He buttoned up his leather jacket and walked away. I didn't call him again. I've heard nothing of him since. I haven't asked. So I don't know if he gave up, moved on, or if he's still out haunting the cities. Maybe he came to see the play. Maybe he's watching this performance. If he is, I hope he likes it. And I hope that whoever's with him, be she the right woman or not, I hope she likes it too.

David Greig

THE RULES OF SEDUCTION

1. ••• BE IN LOVE. •••

YOU ARE ABSOLUTELY INTERESTED IN HER. IN NO ONE OTHER THAN HER. EVERYTHING ABOUT HER HAS BEWITCHED YOU. YOU WANT TO KNOW HER. YOU CANNOT FAKE THIS. THIS HAS TO BE REAL.

2. ••• BE HONEST. •••

IF YOU WANT TO HAVE SEX WITH HER, TELL HER. THERE IS A DIFFERENCE BETWEEN LECHERY AND SEDUCTION. THE LECHER, WHEN HE SAYS, 'I WANT TO FUCK YOU', WANTS TO MAKE THE WOMAN FEEL UNCOMFORTABLE. HE WANTS TO EXPRESS HOW MUCH HE DESPISES HER. WHEN I SAY IT, I MEAN IT. IT CARRIES NO THREAT COMING FROM ME, BECAUSE IT IS AN EXPRESSION OF DESIRE, NEVER AN EXPRESSION OF HOSTILITY.

3. ••• BE SENSUAL. •••

IN YOUR LANGUAGE, IN YOUR THOUGHT, BE ALIVE TO THE FORM OF THINGS. TWO PEOPLE WHO LOOK AT A PAINTING TOGETHER, OR WHO DISCUSS THE SHAPE OF THE ROCKS ON A HILLSIDE, OR WHO ARGUE ABOUT THE MERITS OF A PARTICULAR NOVEL . . . ARE SEDUCING EACH OTHER: THEIR RHETORIC IS THE LANGUAGE OF TOUCH.
NOTE: THERE IS A GLASS FACTORY IN PROVENCE WHERE YOU CAN WATCH THE WORKERS BLOW THE MOLTEN GLASS STRAIGHT FROM THE FURNACE. THIS IS VERY SEDUCTIVE.

4. ••• DON'T BE BEAUTIFUL, BE TALENTED. •••

SERGE GAINSBOURG, GEORGES SIMENON, KEITH RICHARDS, SHELLEY, LORD ROCHESTER, CASANOVA. NONE OF HISTORY'S GREAT LOVERS HAVE BEEN GOOD LOOKING. THEY HAVE ALL BEEN TALENTED.

5. ••• LET YOURSELF BE LOOKED AT. •••

AT SOME MOMENT YOU WILL BE UNSELFCONSCIOUS. YOU WILL ENGAGE YOURSELF IN SOME TASK WHICH WILL ABSORB YOUR

TOTAL ATTENTION. AT THIS POINT SHE'LL LOOK AT YOU AND, WHATEVER HER FEELINGS FOR YOU, SHE WILL FEEL THEM

IN AN INTENSE, DISTILLED FORM. SHE WILL ALWAYS ATTEMPT TO RECOVER THIS MOMENT, THIS FIRST GLIMPSE, BUT

NEVER WILL.

NOTE: THE SAME WORKS IN THE NEGATIVE. THIS COULD BE THE MOMENT SHE LEAVES YOU.

6. ••• PLACE YOURSELF IN THE PRESENCE OF DEATH. •••

FUNERALS, HOSPITALS, TELEVISION NEWS REPORTS OF DISASTER, AIRCRAFT, ROCK CLIMBING.

7. ••• HAVE A REPUTATION. •••

THE PRESENCE OF THE POSSIBILITY OF SEX IS A POWERFUL APHRODISIAC. IF SHE KNOWS ABOUT YOUR REPUTATION, THE

POSSIBILITY HANGS IN THE AIR. ANY DYKE WILL TELL YOU THAT STRAIGHT WOMEN ARE FOREVER PROPOSITIONING OUT

DYKES IN WAYS THEY WOULD NEVER APPROACH CLOSETED WOMEN.

8. ••• UNDERSTAND PLEASURE. •••

SIMPLY BECAUSE THERE ARE OTHER THINGS IN LIFE BESIDES PLEASURE DOES NOT MEAN THAT IT'S SINFUL TO BECOME

EXPERT IN IT. TO KNOW ITS POSSIBILITIES, TO SEEK IT AND TAKE IT WHERE YOU FIND IT

9. ••• NEVER BLAME. •••

NEVER, EVER, EVER TALK ABOUT OTHER WOMEN IN ANYTHING OTHER THAN FLATTERING TERMS. YOU WILL NOT JUDGE HER.

YOU WILL NOT BLAME HER. YOU WILL NOT COMPARE HER.

10. ••• KEEP SECRETS. •••

NOT YOUR OWN. HERS.

Suspect Culture

Suspect Culture are a touring theatre company based in Glasgow, Scotland founded in 1990 by Graham Eatough and David Greig in association with composer Nick Powell. The company is made up of core artistic and administrative staff and a group of long standing artistic associates who together have established a reputation both at home and abroad for producing innovative and accomplished new work.

The company develops projects from concept through workshop to presentation on stage aiming to realise ideas in all elements of the production as well as in the stories told.

Recent productions include:

Mainstream - a performance for four actors playing two characters, who, in the desire to communicate, find that the more they tell the less they reveal. The production premiered in Scotland in 1999 and has since visited London, Dublin, Prague and cities in Croatia, Greece and Bulgaria. A typically immaculate piece of work from the most adventurous, most in-tune-with-the-times theatre company in Britain (**The Times**).

The Golden Ass - a unique collaboration between members of the community from the Gorbals in Glasgow and the company including theatre practitioners from Italy and Brazil. The performance was adapted from the Roman satire by Apuleius to look at issues of wealth and power in today's society. **The Golden Ass** was performed at the Tron Theatre, Glasgow in December 2000. Theatre as it should be: a physical and intellectual thrill, a challenge, and, at times, a puzzle (**The Guardian**).

Timeless - performed with an original score played live by a string quartet, **Timeless** tells the story of four friends whose present past and future lives are delicately intertwined. The production was commissioned as part of the Edinburgh International Festival in 1997 where it won a Scotland On Sunday Critics' Award. That Scotland should have produced Suspect Culture that begat Timeless should make a small nation swell with pride (**The Herald**).

Other productions are: **Candide 2000** (UK 2000), **Airport** (Scotland & Spain 1996; Italy 1997; the Basque Country 1998), **One Way Street** (Scotland 1995; Germany 1997).

As part of on going dramaturgical research, the company also holds an annual symposium titled **Strange Behaviour**. The day-long event pairs theatre with another subject and brings people from both fields for discussions, presentations and workshops. Subjects so far have included sciences of the mind and divinity and participants have included Biyi Bandele, Edwin Morgan, David Jasper, Katie Mitchell, Dan Rebellato, Colwyn Trevarthen, and Mole Wetherell. The next symposium, in December 2001, will pair theatre and mathematics.

Other forthcoming projects include: the **Cranes Project** - a lighting installation on cranes in Dublin's city centre choreographed to an original soundscape broadcast on FM radio (a co-production with Dublin Fringe); and **K2** - a large scale work for theatre inspired by stories of high altitude mountaineering and featuring a ballet of climbers. **K2** will be performed at the Tramway in Glasgow in 2003.

For further information about Suspect Culture please contact -
Suspect Culture
128 Elderslie Street
Glasgow G3 7AW
www.suspectculture.co.uk
[e] suspectculture@btconnect.com
[t] +44 (0)141 248 8052
[f] +44 (0)141 221 4470

Paul Blair as 'Casanova', August 2001

Casanova was first performed at the Tron Theatre, Glasgow in February 2001 with the following cast: Vicki Liddelle as 'Kate,' Louise Ludgate as 'Marie Louise,' Gavin Mitchell as 'Casanova,' Anne Marie Timoney as 'Mrs Tennant,' and Alan Williams as the 'Cabinet Maker.' Suspect Culture would like to thank the original cast whose work and ideas have been invaluable in the development of both this production and this text of **Casanova**.

For their support and assistance with **Casanova**, Suspect Culture would also like to thank:

David Shea, David Sneddon, and David Young for their talents and all their hard work; the Tron Theatre and all its staff; RSAMD; Citizen's Theatre; Mauricio Paroni de Castro and Laura Trevisan; the Archa Theatre and the British Council in Prague; all those who participated in Suspect Culture's Open Workshop in June 2000; Benno Plassman; TAG Theatre Company; 7:84 Theatre Company; Marshall Wilson and QB; Rogano; Glasgow Airport; Vodaphone; Vision Express, Buchanan Galleries.

Hair by DLC

Set made by Scott Associates
Floor made by Mark Harrod
Lighting feature made by J&B Scenery
Floor painted by Caroline Wilson

Production photography by Kevin Low [www.kevinlow.co.uk]
Publicity by Podge Publicity (www.podge.co.uk)
Print design by Patrick Macklin in Lapland (www.inlapland.co.uk)

Louise Ludgate as 'Marie Louise' and Gavin Mitchell as 'Casanova' at the Tron Theatre, February 2001

David Greig
Casanova

A Suspect Culture Text

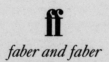

faber and faber

First published in 2001
by Faber and Faber Limited
3 Queen Square, London WC1N 3AU
Published in the United States by Faber and Faber Inc.
an affiliate of Farrar, Straus and Giroux LLC, New York

Typeset by Country Setting, Kingsdown, Kent CT14 8ES
Printed in England by Mackays of Chatham plc, Chatham, Kent

A CIP record for this book
is available from the British Library

ISBN 0-571-21278-6

2 4 6 8 10 9 7 5 3 1

Characters

Casanova
a collector of art

Mrs Tennant
a very wealthy woman

Marie Louise
a personal assistant

Kate
a private detective

The Cabinet Maker

The actress playing Kate also plays

Katrina
an American architect's wife

Eva
a Finnish academic

Carlotta
an Italian Customs officer

Molly
an arts journalist

Kayleigh
a conceptual artist

The Boy Rock Star

The time is the present

CASANOVA

Act One

Act One

ONE: THE PROLOGUE

CASANOVA

There is a war between women and men, and I –
All my life I've been a spy,
Working undercover,
A sexual double agent, and the world's greatest lover.
Don't ask me where my loyalties lie.
It's been so long, I've forgotten now which side I'm on.
I'm a man who loves pleasure, I won't apologise.
In the theatre of sex,
Normal dialogue consists of lies.
And I have never been a liar
(at least not as regards desire).
No, like all good spies, my honesty's been my best disguise.
However, needs must,
Even spies must earn a crust
So I collect art on behalf of a very wealthy patroness.
She's kept me well I must confess.
Her taste's bohemian, contemporary, a little risqué,
And recently she called to say
'I want you to come home, come home and show
The world the secrets that you know.
Describe the battlefield of sex from your perspective.'
So she's arranged a very major retrospective.
On sex.
Where we are and where we're headed.
An account of all the women I have bedded.
It will be a very big exhibition,
An apologia, a guide to making and receiving passes,
Guaranteed to cause a ruction
And excite the chattering classes.

9

My life has been a work of art, I am a man beyond
  the norm.
My sexual success has proved the triumph of content
  over form.
Every one of my seductions is an essay on the human heart
And its complex interaction with the human private part.
Part manifesto, part confession, all absolutely true,
A philosophy of the bedroom from a radical point of view.
My unusual CV will be an exposé
Of those who say
That women don't seek pleasure too.
I will announce a revolution
In human sexual evolution.
To the book of morals I'll set fire,
And declare a republic of desire.
I'll do all that stuff and more,
I'll gladhand like a media whore.
But not yet, not yet, please not just yet . . .
There's still one thing I have to get.
A work of art must have an ending,
And I haven't found my ending yet –
The last lover, a woman who in quality, in look,
Sums up the argument, befits the closing of the book,
Whose very being assaults the moralisers,
Columnists and political advisers,
The puritans who would inhibit sexual freedom –
One last exhibit.
And then, with her beside me, I will expose myself to
  the light,
Be seen, be judged, be crucified and fade into the night.
I'll leave the stage.
I'll disappear, slough off this skin,
Find some remote cottage to live in,
Maybe with a barn to renovate.
I'll make furniture all day,

Smoke, and contemplate the past.
Each breath one nearer to the last.
The revolution will continue,
The war of attrition,
Of caress and kiss,
Of dominance and submission.
But it will go on without me.
To be a spy like Blunt, like Philby,
Is always to know what our final act will be –
To tell.
To tell all.
Be damned.
And go to hell.

TWO

At the airport.
Marie Louise with her little suitcase.
Mrs Tennant seeing her off.

MRS TENNANT
You will be careful, Marie Louise?
He can be very persuasive.

MARIE LOUISE
You've no need to worry about me, Mrs Tennant.

MRS TENNANT
Are you sure?

MARIE LOUISE
He's not the kind of man I'm interested in.

MRS TENNANT
You might be shocked, Marie Louise.
One or two of the things he does, in particular.
You might find them shocking.

MARIE LOUISE

I've had a very catholic education, Mrs Tennant.
I mean that in the broadest sense of the word.
I think I know what depths the human male can sink to.
I don't mind what he does
As long as he doesn't do it in front of me.

MRS TENNANT

He may, Marie Louise. He may 'do it' in front of you.

MARIE LOUISE

He can do what he likes.
He's sick if you ask me.
I feel sorry for him.
Because you must be a very lonely person to do what
he does. You must be a very rejected-feeling person.
You must be a very depressive person if you can't find
true love in the arms of one woman.

MRS TENNANT

I need you to be discreet, Marie Louise.
I want you to assist him in any way that he requires. But
you must not sleep with him.
I need one source of information that I can
completely trust.
That's why I've chosen you to bring him home.
You're strong, you're honest, Marie Louise.
Your heart's a castle. I know I can rely on you.

MARIE LOUISE

Thank you, Mrs Tennant, for your vote of confidence
but you can rest assured that nothing would disgust me
more than the idea of sleeping with that man.
The man I'm looking for will be steady, decent, kind,
spontaneous, loving and good with kids. He will be
kind to his mother and polite to mine (who's ill) but
most of all the man I'm looking for will be totally
utterly and completely in love with me. Only me.

MRS TENNANT

Good.
Now, I've given you credit cards, a lap-top, a web-cam,
a phone – everything you need. Don't let him out of
your sight until he's back here safely in time for the
exhibition.
Is that clear?

MARIE LOUISE

Absolutely, Mrs Tennant.

MRS TENNANT

He'll meet you in Los Angeles airport.

MARIE LOUISE

OK.

MRS TENNANT

Be careful.
Oh.
And Marie Louise – when you see him . . .

MARIE LOUISE

Yes.

MRS TENNANT

Send him my love.

Mrs Tennant leaves.

MARIE LOUISE

Sick.

THREE

In an airport toilet.
    Casanova and Katrina have been fucking.
    Katrina lights a cigarette.
    She shares it with him.

KATRINA

That was fucking fantastic.

CASANOVA

Shhh.

An airport announcement, final call for passengers
    to Denver.

KATRINA

They're calling my flight.

CASANOVA

You should run. Your husband will be looking for you.

KATRINA

Poor Dave.

CASANOVA

Lucky Dave, to have you.

KATRINA

You know what I like about my husband?

CASANOVA

What do you like?

KATRINA

When we catch a plane together, he always reserves the
seats beside the emergency exit. I love that about him.

CASANOVA

He's solid.

KATRINA

As a rock.
He's an architect, you know.

CASANOVA

He sounds like a great guy.

KATRINA

A real winner.

CASANOVA

You should get back to him.

KATRINA

No.

CASANOVA

But he'll be looking for you.

KATRINA

Let him catch the plane alone.
I'm leaving him.

CASANOVA

You're leaving Dave?

KATRINA

Dave's a coffin. Dave's crushing me. I can't breathe
around Dave any more. Dave's a supermassive black
hole sucking the life-blood out of me. I'm never going
back to Dave again.

CASANOVA

Talk to him. Talk it through. You'll work it out.

KATRINA

No. I'm going to disappear for a while.

CASANOVA

Where will you go?

KATRINA

I don't know, maybe the desert.

CASANOVA

What will you do?

KATRINA

Maybe waitressing.

CASANOVA

Is this because of – me?

KATRINA

You, Dave, men. You think the world revolves around you.

CASANOVA

We meet in the café, we have sex in the toilet.
It is, as you say, 'fucking fantastic'.
Now you want to leave your husband, Dave.
Are you saying you want to be with me?

KATRINA

When I saw you looking at me
I didn't want to be with you.
I wanted to have been with you.
Secretly and quickly.
And now I have.
You know what I thought about when we were fucking?

CASANOVA

Dave?

KATRINA

Death.
I thought about being fucked by death.
. . .
Give me your hand.

He does.
She reads his palm.

A Mexican woman taught me to do this.
This is fun. I'm always right.
You have no children
And no wife.
You'll die soon.
Alone.
Gee. Bad hands.

CASANOVA

Does it say what'll kill me?

KATRINA

Oh sure.

> *She opens his shirt.*
> *Takes some lipstick*
> *and marks a cross on his chest.*

Your heart.
. . .
Gotta go.
Nice meeting you.

CASANOVA

Wait . . .
What's your name?

KATRINA

Katrina.

CASANOVA

I'll remember you, Katrina.

KATRINA

Bullshit.
You'll forget me the moment I'm out of your sight.

> *She leaves.*

FOUR

The Cabinet Maker's workshop.
The Cabinet Maker is working.
A likeness of Casanova in the cabinet.

CABINET MAKER

He's not much to look at.
He looks like a fucked-up lesbian singer or something.
But that's what women go for isn't it?
Because this man has –
Some allure he has that good men lack.
You go for that.
You have no understanding of love.
Women – females – and men like him –
No understanding of the responsibility of love.
Which is – work – as a matter of fact.
Hard work
And keeping quiet about it.
That's what love is – and he destroys it.
This is him.

Kate enters.
She is drinking coffee from a paper cup.
She looks at Casanova.

KATE

Is it a good likeness?

CABINET MAKER

It's him.

KATE

OK.

The Cabinet Maker looks at her.

CABINET MAKER

Are you – does he . . .?

18

KATE

What?

CABINET MAKER

Does he – you know –
Does he do it for you?

KATE

Would that bother you?

CABINET MAKER

I knew it.

KATE

He's – interesting.
Everybody's interesting.
You're interesting.
I'm a detective.
People interest me.
The things they want.

CABINET MAKER

Look at him.
Remember him.

KATE

Where is he now?

CABINET MAKER

He's been in America.
Fucking up American lives.
Now he's coming home to stage an exhibition.
I have been employed to build the cabinets.

KATE

OK.
So – I meet him – in the gallery like you said –
I'm disguised as your wife.
Alone.
What next?

CABINET MAKER

You allow yourself to be seduced by him.
You get him to undress.
You get him naked.

KATE

You want me to undress as well?

CABINET MAKER

No.
You're dressed.

KATE

Fine.
Then what?

CABINET MAKER

You love him.
You're besotted. Irrational.
That's what you're like.
He's stolen your heart.

KATE

OK.

CABINET MAKER

And he's aroused.
You're doing everything right so he's aroused.

KATE

Anything in particular?

CABINET MAKER

Teasing.
Teasing things in particular.
You must know what these things are.
You – choose from your repertoire.

KATE

OK.

CABINET MAKER

And then you start to have sex.

KATE

That'll cost you.

CABINET MAKER

I don't want you to do it.
You're about to do it.
Even if you want to – don't.
About to.

KATE

Still costs more.
Any encounters of this type.
I promise you.
Experience tells me they're very difficult to control.
You can't predict how the subject's going to react.

CABINET MAKER

Just when he's losing . . . himself in –
Just at that moment.
Stop.
It's very important you don't get carried away.

KATE

I'll try.

CABINET MAKER

And then you say –
This is what I want you to say –
Say –
'Do you remember me?'

KATE

Do you remember me?

CABINET MAKER

And he'll say –
Something like – 'What?' or . . .

He'll just be confused.
Just ask the question again.
And again.
Until he says – 'No. I don't remember you.'

KATE

What if he doesn't say that?

CABINET MAKER

He will.
He will, and then you'll say,
'The Cabinet Maker remembers.'
'The Cabinet Maker remembers his wife.'
Say that.

KATE

The Cabinet Maker remembers his wife.

CABINET MAKER

With more sadness.
'The Cabinet Maker remembers his wife.'
And then you take out the gun.

KATE

From where?

CABINET MAKER

What?

KATE

Where have I concealed the gun?

CABINET MAKER

I don't know.
In a holster.

KATE

He'll feel it when he caresses my shoulder.

CABINET MAKER

Strap it to your stomach.

KATE

He'll feel it when he caresses my stomach.

CABINET MAKER

Where won't he caress you?

KATE

That's the million dollar question.
Isn't it?

CABINET MAKER

You're the detective.
You hide the gun.

KATE

Find gun. Show gun.
I'm the wife.
You're the bastard.
Remember?
Now you're gonna die.
Point gun at head? Face? Cock?
Yeah?

CABINET MAKER

No. No.

KATE

What?

CABINET MAKER

I want him to say sorry.

KATE

Gun.
To the head.
'Say sorry.'

CABINET MAKER

Apologise.
For what you did.
Apologise for the pain you've caused.

To the Cabinet Maker,
and his wife.
Apologise.

CABINET MAKER

KATE

OK. Say sorry. OK.
You know, for a revenge hit.
That's quite old-fashioned.

CABINET MAKER

An apology will destroy him.
And it will destroy his exhibition.

KATE

OK.
'Sorry, I confess. It was me.'
Then Bang. Dead.

CABINET MAKER

No.
Just leave him.
Leave him alone.

KATE

OK.
It's better if we have some arrangement on paper.
Hire me as your assistant.
You're paying me to help with the cabinets.
I'll work up a price for the hit.
I'll invoice you for half up-front.
Half later.
This is a professional arrangement.
I don't want any confusion.

CABINET MAKER

No confusion from me.
I assure you.

Kate is leaving.

KATE

By the way.
What if he doesn't apologise?
What if he refuses?

CABINET MAKER

Gun to the face. Bang. He's dead.

FIVE

In Los Angeles airport.
  Marie Louise is on her mobile speaking to Mrs Tennant.
  She is holding a sign saying 'Marie Louise'.
  She sits on her suitcase, holding the sign.

MARIE LOUISE

Mrs Tennant, I'm in Los Angeles.
I need a description of him.
I realised when I got off the plane that I don't know what he looks like.
At first I thought if he's as attractive as you say he is then I'll spot him anyway because he'll have a quality, a look that'll set off a spark in me. But I'm looking, Mrs Tennant, and nobody's setting off any sparks.
He may have seduced a thousand women.
But I'm immune.
I'm safe.
Because whichever one of these men he is –
he does nothing for me.

  Casanova enters.
    She sees him.
    She immediately senses who he is.

CASANOVA

Are you waiting for me?

MARIE LOUISE

Yes.

CASANOVA

Marie Louise.
Two beautiful names.
I'm sorry I'm late. I . . . was involved in a moment of
pure undiluted joyful intimacy with a stranger.
I thought you'd understand.
Let me take your case.

Marie Louise stands up.
She talks into the phone.

MARIE LOUISE

Good God.
Sorry.
I was –
Yes.
I just didn't expect.
. . .
It's him.
That's definitely him.

She switches off the phone.

CASANOVA

Quite extraordinary. Quite beautiful. Quite fascinating.

MARIE LOUISE

Who?

CASANOVA

The woman I've just been with.
I could have listened to her for hours.
Married to an architect.
She's run off to be a waitress in the desert.
The poor husband's waiting for her at the gate.
Tears falling on his boarding pass.

MARIE LOUISE

Did you – have sex with her?

CASANOVA

Oh yes.

MARIE LOUISE

Did you collect an exhibit from her?

CASANOVA

Yes.

MARIE LOUISE

Good. The last exhibit. I'll have it sent to Mrs Tennant
and we can start to make arrangements to go home.

CASANOVA

Not the last.

MARIE LOUISE

There's more?

CASANOVA

Just one.

MARIE LOUISE

Where?

CASANOVA

I haven't found her yet.
But I will.

MARIE LOUISE

But Mrs Tennant wants you back home now.

CASANOVA

I'm sure Mrs Tennant wouldn't begrudge us a drink
in the bar before we go?

MARIE LOUISE

I don't drink when I'm working. It's a rule.

CASANOVA

Who said anything about working?
And Marie Louise,
While you're with me – let's not have rules.
What are you having?

MARIE LOUISE

. . .
A long vodka.

They exit.

SIX

The Cabinet Maker's workshop.
The Cabinet Maker is working on a cabinet.
Kate is fitting a petrol canister inside the cabinet.
Mrs Tennant enters.

MRS TENNANT

How long will they take to finish?

CABINET MAKER

It depends. A week, maybe two. Most of the cases are
done.

MRS TENNANT

I need them sooner.

CABINET MAKER

You do keep asking for more.

MRS TENNANT

He's a man of prodigious appetites.

CABINET MAKER

Clearly.

MRS TENNANT

Who's she?

CABINET MAKER

Kate is my new assistant.

MRS TENNANT

Is Kate discreet?
I don't want journalists finding out before we open.

CABINET MAKER

She can keep secrets.

MRS TENNANT

Are the cases strong enough?

CABINET MAKER

They're bullet-proof. Bomb-proof. Earthquake-proof.
Heat, light, or water won't corrode them.
They're absolutely airtight and completely solid.
I have never made a case this strong before.
Long after the building itself has crumbled to dust,
This case and its contents will remain exactly as
they were on the day you opened the gallery.

MRS TENNANT

Good.

KATE

Mrs Tennant, why do the cases have to be so strong?

MRS TENNANT

I'm expecting trouble.
That women fuck strangers, surprisingly, still shocks
some people.
Does it shock you, Kate?

Kate emerges.

KATE

I find it interesting.

MRS TENNANT

Really. I find it arousing.
What about this one. 'The Lebanese Waitress.'
He was in Beirut, one day he was drinking at the
Commodore Hotel with some war correspondents.
Suddenly a car bomb exploded outside four floors
below them. The newspapermen ran down to get
the story. He saw the waitress standing by the
shattered window looking down.
They were taking bodies from the car. The bar was
empty. He stood behind the waitress, put his hand on
her hip. She didn't resist his touch. He lifted her skirt.
She continued to stare at the blood on the tarmac.
Without turning her head she moved her body. Just
slightly, into him. The smell of petrol. He never saw
the woman's face.

KATE

How did he know she wouldn't resist?

MRS TENNANT

He didn't.
Isn't that arousing?

KATE

He was taking a risk.

MRS TENNANT

He knew that a war zone is also an erogenous zone.
The sight of corpses always makes us want to steal back
some life from the pockets of death.

CABINET MAKER

What do you think of the cabinet, Mrs Tennant?

MRS TENNANT

It's perfect.

CABINET MAKER

Good.

MRS TENNANT

Does it upset you, that you build the case, but no one will give you any credit for the work?

CABINET MAKER

There are two worlds, Mrs Tennant. The world of art and the world of Cabinet Makers. In the one they come to look at the art and are indifferent to the cabinets. In the other they come to look at the cabinets and are indifferent to the art. Amongst Cabinet Makers I am . . .

MRS TENNANT

Picasso?

CABINET MAKER

Michelangelo.

MRS TENNANT

Lucky us.
Lucky Kate to have you as a teacher.
You have a week to finish the rest of the cases.

She exits.
    Kate is looking at the cabinet.

CABINET MAKER

The Lebanese Waitress.
What about the Lebanese Waitress's husband?
No doubt he was in the car.

The Cabinet Maker removes the canister from the case.

What are you laughing at?

KATE

. . .
I'm not laughing, I'm smiling.

CABINET MAKER

Smile, if you want,
It must be hard not to smile.
I'm used to it.
The female admiration for the thief.

KATE

If you want me to play your wife.
I'm going to need . . . clothes, photographs.
Something to go on.
What build was she – tall, small . . . ?

CABINET MAKER

Your build.
Not precisely but – in form you . . .
Resemble her.

KATE

Resemblance is not enough.
To convince a man who was once her lover.
I need to inhabit her.
You do understand?

CABINET MAKER

I understand.

KATE

So you'll have to help me bring her to life.
. . .
Do you remember her?

CABINET MAKER

Every detail.

KATE

Tell me.

SEVEN

An airport bar in Los Angeles.
  Casanova and Marie Louise.
  Silence.

MARIE LOUISE

OK.
I'm sorry but I think it's better if we get this out of the
way. You're going to have to stop this right now.
I am not available.
I am not interested.
I am not falling for it.
So you can stop wasting your time.
This – hair flicking, this – eyes looking.
This business of – you know – half-smiles.
This drawing attention to the back of your hands.
Have a drink!
This pure undiluted pleasure this –
Why don't we just
Have a long vodka!
It won't work.
It won't work on me.

CASANOVA

Of course.
We're colleagues.
We can't possibly – even if we wanted –
Express desire.
. . .
It's absolutely – out of bounds.

MARIE LOUISE

So we're clear?

CASANOVA

Clear.

MARIE LOUISE
Right.

CASANOVA
By the way,
Mrs Tennant told me your mother wasn't well.
I hope she's on the mend.

MARIE LOUISE
. . .

CASANOVA
We're not working just now.
Why don't you phone her.
See how she is?

EIGHT

Kate and the Cabinet Maker in the workshop.
  The Cabinet Maker with a wig.
  He puts the wig on Kate.

CABINET MAKER
She wore her hair short,
It was
. . .
(*Closes his eyes.*)
Dark.
The colour of . . .
. . .
Coffee.
. . .
It was
Nearly, but not precisely
This colour.
She didn't smile like that.
. . .

Her smile was . . .
Your neck is –
She had a swan's neck . . . she held her head –
She was . . .

Close your eyes.
Think of her.
The first time you saw her.
What do you see?

NINE

The Airport Bar.
  Casanova and Marie Louise.

CASANOVA

What do you think of her?
The woman in the black – look at her, the way she eats.

MARIE LOUISE

We really should be buying our tickets home.

CASANOVA

Or her, the woman selling flowers.
She likes me.

MARIE LOUISE

She's putting it on so you buy me a rose.
Have you got your passport?

CASANOVA

You know, I'm glad Mrs Tennant sent you.
You're serious.
You have a quality . . .
Like.
Like Joan of Arc.

MARIE LOUISE

Just stop it.

CASANOVA

What?

MARIE LOUISE

This flirting.

CASANOVA

I never flirt.

MARIE LOUISE

I think you're forgetting.
I am sexual asbestos.
Unlike Joan of Arc, I am fireproof.

CASANOVA

She is beautiful.

MARIE LOUISE

Who?

CASANOVA

Oh my God.
. . .
Don't look now.
She's coming this way.

*Eva enters, she is carrying some books under her
arms.*
    She is a Finnish academic.
    *Just as she walks past, Casanova pushes his wine
glass to the floor.*

EVA

I'm so sorry.
Was that my fault?

Both kneel to pick up the glass.

CASANOVA

It was my fault.
I dropped the glass deliberately.

EVA

Why?

CASANOVA

You're the most attractive woman I've ever seen.
I had to get your attention somehow.
I had no choice.
Are you here to meet someone?

EVA

I'm here to meet my girlfriend.

CASANOVA

Leave her, we'll go somewhere.
I know a very sleazy club not far from the airport.
We can take a taxi there now.
Your girlfriend hasn't seen you yet.
We still have time.

EVA

She's seen me.

CASANOVA

Meet me tomorrow. I'll book a hotel.
One night. That's all I ask.
I assure you I'll leave in the morning
and you'll never see my face again.

EVA

I'm leaving for Italy in twenty minutes.

CASANOVA

Cancel the flight.

EVA

I'm going to a conference in Milan.
I can't possibly cancel.

CASANOVA

Are you Italian?

EVA

I'm Finnish, from Helsinki.

CASANOVA

What's your name?

EVA

Eva.

CASANOVA

Eva. Eva.
One night Eva.
One night.

Eva walks off.

MARIE LOUISE

I can't believe you did that.

CASANOVA

She's the one. The one who'll finish the exhibition.
She's perfect.
Marie Louise – book two tickets to Milan.
First class.
Tell Mrs Tennant we've been delayed.
We can sleep on the plane.
I'll meet you in the smokers' lounge.

Casanova exits.

TEN

The Cabinet Maker's workshop.

CABINET MAKER

She is
Standing in a garden, on a green, smooth, lawn.
The sun's shining and she's wearing a summer dress.
I can see the outline of her body under the dress.
She's holding a baby up in the air.
In the background, I can see a wooden fence.
Someone has treated it with creosote.

KATE

OK.
I can see that –
Another picture –
Something more about her.

CABINET MAKER

We're getting married.
In the rain.
In a church on a moor . . .

KATE

I see the church.
I see the moor.
I still can't see her.

CABINET MAKER

Her hair is black, her neck is like a swan . . .
I've stopped at restaurant windows and stared
Because a woman's hair seemed like hers.
I've followed women down alleys because they
walk in a way that reminds me of her.
I've stared at a woman until she became afraid
because an expression she had might just
have been one of hers.

But the moment I see her . . .
She disappears.
. . . the woman remains, the form
but she's still gone.

KATE
It's OK. It's all right.

CABINET MAKER
I can see the lawn, I can smell the creosote.

KATE
Lets start with something solid, something real.

CABINET MAKER
This was hers. She left it.

He gives her the dress.
She puts it on.
She looks in a mirror.

KATE
She's young.
Younger than you.
Beside you she seems – blank.
Not much of a woman.
. . .
You could break into a heart like that,
As easy as taking a car.

CABINET MAKER
If someone had stolen my car, I would have gone to the
police. Maybe it would even have been returned to me.
Undamaged.
And I would still be driving it.
Listening to CDs, changing gear.
He did not destroy my faith in cars.

KATE

Look, I still need more.
I need to understand her.
I'm going to go to the gallery.
There are things I need to find out.

CABINET MAKER

Wait.

KATE

What?

CABINET MAKER

Your eyes.
Your eyes are just like her eyes.

KATE

Good. Eyes.
That's enough for today.
We'll continue tomorrow.

Kate exits.

ELEVEN

Milan Airport.
Casanova is waiting with a suitcase.
He is looking at Carlotta, an Italian customs officer.
Marie Louise enters.

MARIE LOUISE

OK. I've booked us a room.
You wouldn't believe the hassle.
The city's full of fashion people.
It's fashion week – apparently.
Every room's full.

I found a place eventually.
I had to pull all kinds of strings.
It's costing a fortune.
We've got connecting rooms. I'm keeping the key to the connecting door by the way.
In case you get any ideas.
There's a fax and a phone line.
I'll have to call Mrs Tennant when we get through customs.

CASANOVA

I need you to be honest, Marie Louise.
How do I look?
Do I look jet-lagged? Do I look old?

MARIE LOUISE

You look fine. Why?

CASANOVA

I feel old.

Casanova moves through customs.
  Carlotta beckons him.
  He puts his bag on the counter.
  He opens it, she looks inside.
  He writes a note.
  He passes it to her.
  She looks at it.
  She writes something.
  She passes it back.
  She closes Casanova's bag.
  He leaves.

CASANOVA

I've found her.
The one.

MARIE LOUISE

Eva? I thought she got the earlier flight?

Not Eva.
Another one.
I just saw her.

MARIE LOUISE

We've barely touched Italian soil.

CASANOVA

I know.
But it's true.
The one turns out to be another one.

TWELVE

The Gallery
Mrs Tennant enters with Kate.
A case full of autumn leaves.

MRS TENNANT

This is the space.
One thousand and one cabinets arranged in the space.
Each cabinet is an object from a different woman.
The last cabinet is empty.

KATE

What's in this one?

MRS TENNANT

Case number one. His first.

KATE

Who was she?

MRS TENNANT

Me.

KATE

Oh.

MRS TENNANT

Which part of that surprises you?

KATE

I don't know.
Your name, you're married I suppose.

MRS TENNANT

I was sixteen.

KATE

He seduced you?

MRS TENNANT

I seduced him.
He was a new boy.
He sat in front of me in the classroom.
He was quiet. Never spoke in class.
But somehow he brought possibility with him whenever
he walked into the room.
One day I passed a note to him.
He opened it and read it.
'Who are you?' it said.
He turned and I was looking at him.
I taught him that.
When he says it to you, it's as if he knows that there's
something infinitely valuable in you and he wants to
mine it, extract it and give it back to you.

KATE

It sounds very calculating.

MRS TENNANT

Oh no. He means it.
We fucked that morning in the warmth of the boiler room
at breaktime. That afternoon on a bed of leaf-litter in
the woods behind the school. That night he climbed the
drainpipe to my bedroom window. Jumping across roofs
to find me.

44

Waking me with a touch.

. . .

In the village they sat at bus stops and took tranquillisers.
They took off their shoes on new carpet. They walked
towards the crematorium gates holding flowers.
But that day, when we fucked.
We tore the village open.
And found the city behind it.

KATE

You didn't stay with him.

MRS TENNANT

My boyfriend beat him up.
Quite badly.
He left after that.

KATE

You said the last cabinet is to be empty.

MRS TENNANT

Yes.
He's saving that one.

KATE

What's going to be in it?

MRS TENNANT

The perfect woman.

KATE

His perfect woman?

MRS TENNANT

A woman with whom he has had the ultimate, absolute
transcendent experience of liberated sex
A woman who is prepared to stand with him, in the
empty box and face the gaze of strangers.

KATE

What if the ultimate, transcendent experience of
liberated sex is only achievable after fifteen years of
married intimacy. Is that possible?

MRS TENNANT

No.

KATE

The last cabinet. Where is it to go?
I need to take measurements for the Cabinet Maker.

MRS TENNANT

You should really meet him. You'd like him.

KATE

What does 'perfect' mean in terms of size?

MRS TENNANT

About your size.

Mrs Tennant's phone rings.

MRS TENNANT

Excuse me.
My assistant's calling.
I have to take it.

Kate starts measuring for the last cabinet.

THIRTEEN

A hotel room in Milan.
Marie Louise unpacking her suitcase.
She is on the phone.

MARIE LOUISE

Mrs Tennant, there's a new exhibit.
One thousand and one.

MRS TENNANT

Where are you?

MARIE LOUISE

Milan.

MRS TENNANT

You're supposed to be on a plane to Heathrow.
What the hell are you doing in Milan?

MARIE LOUISE

He's chasing a woman.

MRS TENNANT

I have the press booked. The whole thing's ready to go.
Bring him home.

MARIE LOUISE

She's perfect he says.

MRS TENNANT

Fuck that.
Who's the new one?

MARIE LOUISE

An architect's wife in the airport toilet.

MRS TENNANT

A toilet?

MARIE LOUISE
The Gents in international arrivals.

MRS TENNANT
God that's beautiful.

MARIE LOUISE
He said she told him his heart would kill him.

MRS TENNANT
Time stolen, pleasure stolen in an airport toilet.
. . .
What was her name?

MARIE LOUISE
I don't know. He never said.

MRS TENNANT
Ask him.
Ask him now.
I want to know.

MARIE LOUISE
Hold on.

Marie Louise opens the connecting door.
    In the other room, Casanova and Carlotta are in bed.
    Carlotta is flicking through the channels.

Good God.
Who's she?

MRS TENNANT
I think we can safely assume that she is
Case number one thousand and two.

FOURTEEN

Casanova and Carlotta. She is switching channels.

CARLOTTA
This is my favourite show.
(*Flick.*)
I love this guy.
He does this quiz.
I never get the answers.
(*Flick.*)
How old are you?

CASANOVA
Why do you ask?

CARLOTTA
You're maybe the oldest guy I've fucked.

CASANOVA
Probably.

CARLOTTA
You're OK.

CASANOVA
Thank you.

CARLOTTA
I don't like men.
Look at that, look at what they're doing – Jesus.
Jesus.
(*Flick.*)

CASANOVA
You like women?

CARLOTTA
I like cats.
And hot baths.

Men want to be fed all the time.
That's why I like you – all this time, you haven't asked
me for any food.
I cook enough for my little boy.

Casanova is going through her stuff. He finds the gun.
He strokes her back with the gun, very gently.

CARLOTTA

You have a lovely touch.

CASANOVA

If you had to, would you kill me?

CARLOTTA

Why?

CASANOVA

You're a police officer. You have a gun.

CARLOTTA

Every man I meet wants me to kill them with my gun.
Jesus Christ.
What is it – you want me to stick it up your arse?

CASANOVA

I don't want you to go away, Carlotta, I feel as though,
the moment I take my hand away from your skin,
I'll disappear.

CARLOTTA

Don't go sentimental on me, old man.
I'm not your mistress.
You go back to whatever wife you have.
Let her cook for you.
I don't want jewels, or dresses.
Does this room have a bath?

CASANOVA

Of course.
Let me take a picture of you?

CARLOTTA

In the bath? Are you a pervert?

CASANOVA

No . . . I just want a portrait.

CARLOTTA

I do undercover work.
Nobody gets my picture.
It's not possible.

CASANOVA

Give me something then. Something uniquely yours.
Something only for me.

CARLOTTA

I already gave you something.

CASANOVA

What?

CARLOTTA

I'll show you.

*She musses up the ash in the ashtray, then she spreads
the ash over the glass table. Then she blows the ash
away. It leaves marks.*

See,
I left my fingerprints everywhere.
Evidence.
Cop kisses.
If a cop leaves her prints, you know she likes you.

*Casanova takes a sheet of paper and lays it down on
the prints. The ash marks the paper.*

CARLOTTA

You're a nice guy, old man.
I like your smile.
But don't get me wrong.

I'm playing a game.
This is pure pleasure for me.
OK.
Warm your cockles somewhere else.
I'm going to have a bath.

She looks in the mirror.

Sex is good for me.
My skin's glowing.
My eyes are bright.
My mind is focused.
Today I will be an excellent servant of the law.
I should have sex more often.

Carlotta leaves.
Marie Louise enters.

MARIE LOUISE
She seems nice.

CASANOVA
Were you watching?

MARIE LOUISE
Only at the end.
Sweet.
Is she the one?

CASANOVA
No.
I thought so but no.

MARIE LOUISE
She could still be. If you got to know her.

CASANOVA
No.

MARIE LOUISE
You know I think you're wicked.

CASANOVA

I know.

MARIE LOUISE

I want you to stop.

CASANOVA

Why?

MARIE LOUISE

I don't want you to be wicked.
I've realised that deep down you're a kind person.
You're just misguided.
Are you hungry?
You look hungry.
Let's eat.

CASANOVA

We haven't time.
I've already missed Eva once.
I got distracted by the cop.
Eva's the one.
I'm going to find her.

MARIE LOUISE

You're going to go to hell.

CASANOVA

Almost certainly, Marie Louise, but not tonight.
Tonight you and I are going to Helsinki.
You'd better have this.

He gives her the fingerprints.

It's the next exhibit.
Send it to Mrs Tennant.
Tell her . . .
Not yet, not just yet.

FIFTEEN

The Cabinet Maker and Kate.
  Kate is wearing the dress and the wig.
  She is carrying a bottle of malt whisky, wrapped in paper.

KATE

Happy birthday.

CABINET MAKER

How did you know?

KATE

I have to know everything about my clients.
I know things even they don't know.
I know you like whisky.
I brought you an invoice.
Half the money up-front.
You ought to check it.

CABINET MAKER

Not now.
Let's . . . let's . . .
I could take you to – are you hungry?
You –
Have you eaten?

KATE

It's OK.
We'll have a drink.

CABINET MAKER

Yes. Good idea. A drink.

He opens the bottle.

KATE

I tracked him down.
I thought
You'd be interested.
It took time.
He's in Milan.
Chasing a woman there.
She's a cop.

CABINET MAKER

Poor woman.

KATE

Do you want me to go there?
Confront him.
It could speed things along.

CABINET MAKER

No.
It has to be here.
I . . .
I've been meaning to say.
Looking at this invoice.
I'm not sure . . .
I don't want the gun involved.
Not any more.

KATE

Why not?

CABINET MAKER

There's nowhere to put it.
And . . .
You might get hurt.

KATE

I'll be all right.
I know how to handle myself.

CABINET MAKER

You –
You look –

KATE

Thank you.

CABINET MAKER

I'm sorry.
Have a drink.

   He pours.

CABINET MAKER

To –
What shall we drink to?
To you?

KATE

To a successful project.

CABINET MAKER

Yes.
. . .
You know, I didn't even know myself,
That today was my birthday.
Until you said.

KATE

I came to check the look.
I've been working on it.
Is it her?
Is it right?

CABINET MAKER

. . .

KATE

It's not right.

CABINET MAKER

It's different.
It's . . . she was . . .

KATE

Say.

CABINET MAKER

She was . . . my wife was
Perfect.
I suppose.

KATE

OK.
That's OK.

CABINET MAKER

I'm sorry.

KATE

Attraction exists in tiny details.
I haven't got the detail right.
That's what you're telling me.
I need more to go on.
. . .
. . .
How am I supposed to do the fucking job
If you can't remember what the fuck she looked like?

CABINET MAKER

I'm sorry. I'll . . .

KATE

Try harder.
I've got to go.

CABINET MAKER

Please, stay, finish your drink.

KATE

I'm on another job.

CABINET MAKER

When will I see you?

KATE

When you've got something I can work on.

SIXTEEN

Casanova and Marie Louise in Helsinki.
Standing outside Eva's apartment.

MARIE LOUISE

I'm freezing.
It must be ten below.
Are you not cold?
You must be cold.

CASANOVA

Her light's on.

MARIE LOUISE

She's gay.
She's a gay Finn.
She's not interested.

CASANOVA

Eva!
Eva! It's me.

MARIE LOUISE

She won't hear you, they'll have double-glazing.

CASANOVA

Eva!
She's at the window.

MARIE LOUISE

C'mon we'll go back to the hotel.
There's a sauna.
You can pick up somebody in the sauna. It'll be much
warmer.

CASANOVA

I don't want anyone else.
I only want her.
She's perfect.

MARIE LOUISE

All Scandinavian women are perfect.
There'll be another one along in a minute.

CASANOVA

Eva,
Let me in.
I have to see you.
I'll die out here.
I'll freeze on your doorstep.
I won't leave.
Unless I hear.
From your own lips.
That you don't want me.

MARIE LOUISE

For God's sake.

CASANOVA

You're laughing at me.

MARIE LOUISE

You're being ridiculous.

CASANOVA

I don't think it's funny.
This is life or death.

MARIE LOUISE

Give up.

CASANOVA

Never.

MARIE LOUISE

You will.

CASANOVA

I won't.

MARIE LOUISE

Sick.
You're sick.
In here – and down there.
I don't understand.

CASANOVA

I need her.

MARIE LOUISE

You need your hole.
Why can't you tell the difference?

CASANOVA

I need her.

MARIE LOUISE

. . .
She's at the window again.
. . .

Eva's voice through an intercom.

EVA

Come on up.

A door entry buzzes
A door opens.
Casanova enters.

Where are you going?
What about me?
What am I supposed to do?
Where am I supposed to go?

Marie Louise is left in the cold.

SEVENTEEN

Kate's flat.
  Kate is in her dressing-gown.
  The Cabinet Maker enters wearing a raincoat.
  Carrying a polythene bag.

KATE

It's late.

  The Cabinet Maker has brought the whisky.
    He gives it to her.

You'd better come in.

  He sits.

It's pouring with rain.
You could have waited till the morning.

  He empties the polythene bag over the floor.
    *It is full of small, pathetic personal objects that she
  left.*

CABINET MAKER

This is her.
This is my wife.
This is all I have.

EIGHTEEN

Casanova in Eva's sauna.
  Eva enters with the whisky.
  She is chewing gum.

EVA

You should meet my girlfriend,
You'd like her.
She'd like you.
Wouldn't it be typical of us Finns,
To both be fucking you?
Separately – each thinking the other doesn't know.
Maybe you are.
Are you?

CASANOVA

I only want you.

EVA

Let me ask you something.
Of all the women you've slept with
How do I compare?
Am I good?

CASANOVA

Very.

EVA

Which percentile am I in?
Tell the truth.

CASANOVA

I've never been happier than at this moment with you.

EVA

Liar.

CASANOVA

I'm telling you the truth.

EVA

So I'm in the top percentile.

CASANOVA

You're in a class of your own.
Kiss me.

EVA

Not yet.
I've still got gum in my mouth.
You know what's interesting?
You're good.
You're even very good.
But curiously, you're not amazing.

CASANOVA

Take off the robe.

EVA

No.
Having sex with you is different from having sex with
my girlfriend.
But it's not a difference in kind.
It's a difference in degree.

CASANOVA

Are you disappointed?

EVA

I'm curious.
Kiss me.
Here.
Now.

CASANOVA

Your girlfriend might come in.

EVA

Do it.

He kisses her.
She stops it.

EVA

Wait, I have to take my gum out.
I'm giving up smoking for my girlfriend.
So I chew this gum as a substitute.
It tastes of shit.

She takes out the gum and puts it down.
They kiss.
Again she stops.

EVA

When I'm with you, I'm not myself any more.
You want nothing from me.
You make me shapeless.
When I'm with you I'm capable of anything.
You.
You're a drug.
Fortunately I'm not addicted to you.

CASANOVA

Stay with me.

EVA

You knew saying that would excite me.

CASANOVA

I mean it – stay with me for a while . . .
only me and only you.

EVA

It's intriguing.
Do you practise this?

CASANOVA

No.

EVA

Do you plot, or plan?
Like a general organising a campaign?

CASANOVA

There's no plan.
I want to be with you.
To feel the shape of your body.
The heat of your breath on me.
I'm afraid of what will happen to me when you go.
That's all.

EVA

I have to go.

CASANOVA

Please.

EVA

I would like to stay.
But I'm going to the desert tomorrow.
I've accepted an invitation to lecture on Proust at the
University of Nevada.
I should really read the book.

She leaves.
    He takes the chewing gum from the bench.

NINETEEN

Kate's flat.
*   The Cabinet Maker is holding a small model of a*
Volkswagen Beetle.

CABINET MAKER

She said I was a weight.
A stone chained to her ankle.
She would dress up like a teenager and go out at night.
If I waited up for her,
She would attack me, drunk, scratching my face.
Accusing me of trying to smother her.
At night I lay beside her,
And gazed at her sleeping.
Delicate and tender.
I would think of waking her with a kiss.
But I wouldn't, because the lightest kiss of mine
Would be too heavy.
. . .
Other times she'd wake me in the early morning.
And dress me quickly.
And drag me out into the fields behind the house,
And we'd sit together watching our breath form clouds
In the dawn light.
Counting the birds.
. . .
She stayed in bed for days on end, weeping, dead.
. . .
She'd buy champagne and get wildly drunk
And demand that we dance.
It didn't matter where we were, or that it was raining.
Or that I can't dance.
Can't even move my legs.
. . .
She would cook me endless meals.

Meals of twelve or fifteen courses.
She would smoke, and watch me as I ate.
Asking me to describe how each dish tasted.

. . .

I hired a detective to have her followed.
I sent her to a psychiatrist.
I got drugs to cure her.
I found a woman to keep her company in the day.
A cleaner, a gardener, a chauffeur and a personal
shopper.

. . .

One summer she went to Europe,
And visited the sites of massacres and church burnings.

. . .

But we were happy.
We were very very happy.

. . .

She met him in an art gallery.
He said he was a curator.
She was my assistant, we were exhibiting somewhere.
And he bought a piece.

. . .

The first time they slept together she was out of her
mind on Bombay Gin.

. . .

She – and – he – and – it – it – she –

. . .

She stood in the living room of the cottage.
Dripping wet from the rain.
And told me that it was best we never saw each other
again.
That I was a black hole.
Sucking her in.
Draining her.
Emptying her of life.
I said – he's put these ideas into your head.

He's filled you up with this.
She said he was the key
That opened the lock
And now the door was swinging open
And she was going to walk through.
. . .
She packed a bag and drove away.
A few days later, they found her car
In the long-stay car park at the airport.
. . .
This is the type of car.
She drove.

> The Cabinet Maker on the floor amongst his wife's
> belongings.

CABINET MAKER

This is the scent she wore.
This is her lipstick.
This is a book she read.
These are the cigarettes she smoked.
This is the music she used to listen to.
. . .
Something you can work with.

TWENTY

Helsinki Airport.
  Casanova and Marie Louise.

MARIE LOUISE

Where are we going now?
Iceland? Bermuda?

CASANOVA

Frankfurt.

MARIE LOUISE

Great.
Fancy a bit of German skirt do you?
Some fräulein with weird-shaped glasses caught your eye?
Don't mind me.

CASANOVA

We're going to Frankfurt to catch a connection home.

MARIE LOUISE

Via the toilets?

CASANOVA

You're upset with me?

MARIE LOUISE

Frostbite.
I had a very cold night looking for a hotel.

TWENTY-ONE

Kate's flat.
  The Cabinet Maker and Kate.

KATE

Run at me.

CABINET MAKER

. . .

KATE

Try to knock me down.

CABINET MAKER

Why?

KATE

Do it.

CABINET MAKER

I'm too heavy.
I'll hurt you.

KATE

Do it.

CABINET MAKER

I'll wind you, I'll knock you out.

KATE

Run hard at me.
Try to hurt me.
Put all your weight behind it.

> *He runs at her and she throws him, powerfully away*
> *from her. He is floored, stunned. He remains on the*
> *floor while Kate picks up the Cabinet Makers wife's*
> *objects, her scent, her lipstick and so on. She examines*
> *them all.*

Kate approaches the Cabinet Maker.
Kneels beside him.
Caresses him.

KATE

She was weak.
I'm strong.

TWENTY-TWO

On an aeroplane.
  Marie Louise and Casanova.

MARIE LOUISE

Sometimes I read a novel, or I watch a film, or I read
a women's magazine, or I just watch how women behave
and I feel embarrassed at them. The stupidity of what
they're supposed to enjoy. The slop they're served up.
The way they put on drag.
They stand like dummies in the window.
The way they simper and whine.
And nod like puppets when a man speaks.
And the way they can never seem to get it together
to actually do anything.
. . .
And men.
The most sensitive, boyish, playful, caring,
good with kids, hard-working, dignified man . . .
Deep down is a dog.
Pawing away at his own genitals.
Lapping at troughs of alcohol.
Battering small creatures.
Fingering himself whenever a schoolgirl walks past.
Crying for his mother.
It's as if men's skulls are bone the whole way through.
. . .

71

I hate you.
You behave as though everything is a pleasure.
As though there's nothing difficult.
Nothing complicated in the world.
No choices.
No God. For example.
For a start.
No God.
Nothing exists for you except a kiss,
A hand in a surprising place,
A fumble in a cupboard,
A tongue across a thigh,
A hand held on a breast,
An unzipped dress falling to the floor.
. . .
So – was she 'the one'?
The Brainy Finn?
Was she perfect?

CASANOVA

No.

MARIE LOUISE

So.
You're still looking?

CASANOVA

No.
. . .
I've found her.

MARIE LOUISE

Who?

CASANOVA

You.

Marie Louise laughs.

MARIE LOUISE

When you're with her, the one,
What will you want from her?

CASANOVA

Something only she can give me.
She alone, and no other woman.

MARIE LOUISE

What can she give you?
Her alone.

CASANOVA

A moment.
Where our eyes lock.
Intimately joined
And we both know.

MARIE LOUISE

What do you both know?

CASANOVA

That we're going to die.
But not yet.

MARIE LOUISE

And what do you, what will you give her?

CASANOVA

Pleasure.

MARIE LOUISE

How do you know you give her pleasure?

CASANOVA

I'm very good at it.

MARIE LOUISE

And she . . . she can just . . .

CASANOVA

Whatever she wants.

MARIE LOUISE

Does she feel bad afterwards?
Does she feel used, abandoned, cheap, soiled?

CASANOVA

Why should she?
There's been no deceit.

MARIE LOUISE

Will she feel guilty?

CASANOVA

She's taken some time, a moment, she's refused to give to
death and she's kept it for herself instead.
Why guilty?

MARIE LOUISE

I want you to know.
I've decided to resign.
I can't concentrate on work when I'm surrounded by
the possibility of sex.
I quit.

CASANOVA

I accept your resignation.

MARIE LOUISE

OK. Good.

TWENTY-THREE

Kate's flat.
  The Cabinet Maker on the floor.
  Kate with him.

KATE

Energy directed towards me
I absorb, and direct to my own advantage.
Forces move through me,
I'm one with the forces in the room.
There's no inside to me and no outside, I contain
nothing.
I'll stop him.
No matter what he throws at me.
He won't defeat me.
Because I have no borders to be penetrated.
No walls to be demolished.
No skin to be pierced.

TWENTY-FOUR

On an aeroplane.
  Casanova and Marie Louise.

MARIE LOUISE

. . .
So I'm going to the loo now,
At the back of the plane.
Where it's quiet.

  She leaves the seat.
    A moment.
    He follows her.

  Interval.

Act Two

Act Two

ONE

Kate's flat, morning.
  The Cabinet Maker and Kate in bed.

KATE

We shouldn't have done that.
It was unprofessional of me,
And unethical.
It was –

CABINET MAKER

. . . You're perfect.

KATE

I should have predicted this outcome.
And avoided it.
Deflected it.

CABINET MAKER

Perfect.
I –
Had forgotten what it feels like – to feel this . . .
This feeling of –

KATE

I'm not her.

CABINET MAKER

. . . you leaving.

KATE

I'm not.

CABINET MAKER

You leaving the bed.

79

The warmth left on the sheet.
To be precise.
I remember it from –

KATE

I'm Kate. Kate now.
Look at me.

The Cabinet Maker looks at her.

CABINET MAKER

Stay. For a while longer.

KATE

I have to go to work.

CABINET MAKER

Of course.

KATE

I'll see you later.

CABINET MAKER

Of course you will.

KATE

I promise.

CABINET MAKER

I believe you.

KATE

I will.

She leaves.

TWO

Frankfurt airport.
  Marie Louise and Casanova outside the smoking lounge.

MARIE LOUISE
The connection's in an hour.
We have to go to gate twelve.

CASANOVA
I don't want to go home.
I want to smoke.

MARIE LOUISE
We have to go home.

CASANOVA
I want a fag.

MARIE LOUISE
I know.

CASANOVA
They're all on tranquillisers at home, you know.
All of them.
They wouldn't know life if it bit them.

MARIE LOUISE
You can teach them.
You'll be famous.

CASANOVA
I'll be finished.

MARIE LOUISE
Would that be so bad?

CASANOVA
. . .

A rest.
It would do you good.
The state of you.

. . .

If you don't mind me saying.

CASANOVA

I'm just tired. Physically.
I'll be fine.
You can't smoke on the flight.
It's three hours.
Where's the smoking lounge?

MARIE LOUISE

It's there, in that glass box.

CASANOVA

Not content with segregating smokers
They want to put us on display as well.
As examples of disease I suppose.
Why don't they just hang up a lung?

MARIE LOUISE

Look – why don't we . . . go for a coffee?
Talk.
The flight's only an hour away.
We don't have long.

CASANOVA

You're beautiful. You're the one. You.

. . .

That woman.
In the lounge, blowing smoke rings.

MARIE LOUISE

No.

CASANOVA

Yes.

MARIE LOUISE

You can't.

CASANOVA

Why not.

MARIE LOUISE

There isn't time.

CASANOVA

Make time, Marie Louise, make time.

Casanova exits.

THREE

The Gallery.
Mrs Tennant enters, speaking to Molly, off stage, and to another journalist on her mobile phone.

MRS TENNANT
(*Dialogue on phone in intalics.*)
I know the exhibition will cause offence.
I want it to cause offence.
It's a political gesture.
(*To Molly.*) There's a press pack on the table.
The problem with politics in this country is that it is not offensive enough.
Photos, biographies, contact numbers, everything you should need.
. . .
I particularly want Christians to protest.
I am delighted that the Cardinal has called for a ban.

Molly enters, she has a press photo of Casanova and a notebook.

MOLLY

He doesn't look the way I'd expected.

MRS TENNANT

I vet all the questions.

MOLLY

I really want to speak to him personally.

MRS TENNANT

What's the format? – I don't want a stitch-up.

MRS TENNANT

I think he makes an excellent role model for
schoolchildren.
Yes, you can quote that.

MOLLY

Oh God, Mrs Tennant, no stitch-ups – no it's just a very
simple interview.
It's a sort of heaven and hell concept.

MRS TENNANT

It is not erotica.
For God's sake don't use that word.
Christ.
Nothing is less erotic than erotica.
Don't you think?
Heaven and Hell?

MOLLY

So – for example, 'What's your idea of heaven?'

MRS TENNANT

No. He's not sad.

MOLLY

'What song's playing in heaven?'

MRS TENNANT

He's very happy.
And everyone he's ever slept with is happy as well.

MOLLY

'Who's with you in heaven?'

MRS TENNANT

Erotica?
It's a slightly nylon concept don't you think?
I'd rather you called it porn.

MOLLY

'What's your idea of hell?'

MRS TENNANT

The council can withdraw funding if they want.
Good, fine – do it.
Ring him, arrange a meeting – that's the number.

MOLLY

He looks sweet.

MRS TENNANT

It's a picture. It doesn't capture –

MOLLY

Like a wee boy.

MRS TENNANT

I don't give a monkeys toss what the city council think.
And neither should you. They're all into bondage and
SM – the councillors. Didn't you know that? Its common
knowledge.Foot fetishists to a man.

MOLLY

He was brought up by his mum wasn't he?

MRS TENNANT

Yes.

MOLLY

Aww.

MRS TENNANT

Excuse me – I've got another call – could you hold.

MOLLY

You can see that. In the picture.
In his eyes. There's a distance.

MRS TENNANT

Hello hon. Where are you?

MOLLY

Is his mother still alive?

MRS TENNANT

No.

MRS TENNANT

I'm just finishing up here. Yeah.
How was your day?

MOLLY

Poor guy.

MRS TENNANT

Really.
Never mind.
Take an aspirin.

MOLLY

No wonder he's all over the place.

MRS TENNANT

Did you stop by at your mother's.
How is she?

MOLLY

He's running away.

MRS TENNANT

Good. That's Good.
Hold on a sec.

MOLLY

You can see it so clearly.
He wants to stop.

MRS TENNANT

What?

MOLLY

I'm just saying.

MRS TENNANT

Ask him what colour his socks are and leave it at that.
OK.
Hello. Yes. I'm back. One last question then.
Make it quick please.

MOLLY

No – of course – like I say – It's a simple format.

MRS TENNANT

We need this exhibition now because this country is
cold and mean and ashamed, and repressed, and violent
and . . . straight.

MOLLY

But you can't help wondering . . .

MRS TENNANT

This is a country that badly needs a fuck.
Yes.
Goodbye.

MOLLY

You can't help wondering what the pain is.

MRS TENNANT

Pain?

Hello again, hon.
Sorry about that.
Yeah.
What do you mean, pain?

MOLLY

His pain. His . . . loss. You know. His mother, or . . .
some lover . . . or . . . an ache.

MRS TENNANT

Oh good. That's good.
An ache?
We'll just watch some crap film on telly.
Yeah.

MOLLY

We all have an ache. Don't we?

MRS TENNANT

Call for a takeaway or something.
Curry.

MOLLY

An inner ache.
I mean god. I have one. Don't you?

MRS TENNANT

Socks. Breakfast. Songs he sings in the shower.
No questions about aches.
Sign this.

MOLLY

What is it?

MRS TENNANT

A confidentiality agreement.
Whatever, hon. You choose.
I'll see you later.
Bye, honey.
Yeah me too.

Molly has signed the agreement. She gives it back.

MOLLY
You know it's funny, but looking at him . . .

MRS TENNANT
If you don't mind, Milly.

MOLLY
Molly.

MRS TENNANT
I'm quite busy here, Molly, so – if you have what you
need.

MOLLY
Looking at him, you can't help but think.
He's had a thousand lovers
And yet
What he really needs is a woman.

Molly exits.

MRS TENNANT
There goes one thousand and four.

The phone rings again.

MRS TENNANT
Marie Louise.
Thank Christ. Where the hell have you been?
I've got interviews set up and everything.
Where is he?

FOUR

Frankfurt Airport.
  Outside the smoking lounge.
  Marie Louise on the phone to Mrs Tennant.

MARIE LOUISE

I'm in Frankfurt Airport.
He's in the smoking lounge.
He's – there's a woman . . .
I don't think he'll want to talk to you.
She's the one.
He's putting his hand under the table, on her knee.
It's – between her legs.
She's –
The slut.
Can't anyone else see them?
It's as though they're invisible.
Is it just me?
In public.
Shameless.
In front of . . .
They're cloaked in smoke and . . .

  She switches the phone off.
    She watches.

FIVE

The airport smoking lounge. Casanova with Kayleigh.
Marie Louise outside, sitting on the luggage.
Casanova lights a fag. Inhales.

CASANOVA

Christ I needed that.

Kayleigh takes the cigarette from him.

KAYLEIGH

I mostly don't smoke.
In Chelmsford everybody smokes.
I only smoke when I'm in airports.
If I can't have it, I want it.
That's me all over.

CASANOVA

What's your name?

KAYLEIGH

Kayleigh.

CASANOVA

Where does that name come from?
Is it from Ireland?

KAYLEIGH

It's from Marillion.
It's my stage name.

CASANOVA

You're an actress?

KAYLEIGH

I'm an artist.

CASANOVA

Really?

KAYLEIGH

Don't sound so surprised.

CASANOVA

Not at all.

KAYLEIGH

You fucker.
You don't believe me.
Fucker.

CASANOVA

What brings you to Frankfurt, Kayleigh?

KAYLEIGH

It's a project.
I can't tell you too much about it.

CASANOVA

What sort of project?

KAYLEIGH

Art.
You cunt.

CASANOVA

What sort of art do you make?

KAYLEIGH

I pretend to be people.

CASANOVA

I'm a curator . . . I curate exhibitions.

KAYLEIGH

You dirty fucker.
You are a dirty old man.

CASANOVA

Do you have a dealer?

KAYLEIGH

Not an art dealer.

CASANOVA

Do you sell your work?

KAYLEIGH

I don't sell it.

CASANOVA

How do you live?

KAYLEIGH

I work. Waitress. Detective. Strip. Temp. DJ. That sort
of thing.

CASANOVA

You document what you do?
That's the art – the different jobs?

KAYLEIGH

You nosy cunt.
You know what I'd like to do?
I'd like to get some coke
And rub it on your dick
And have you fuck me again. ·
How'd you like that?

CASANOVA

I suspect I would enjoy it enormously.
But I have a plane to catch.
I have to go home.

KAYLEIGH

The way you smoke.
Smoking like that.
Like some poof.
You prefer it with boys?
Is that what this is all about?
Think I look like a fucking boy?

CASANOVA

I didn't realise it was an unusual way to smoke.

KAYLEIGH

Fucking unusual in Chelmsford.
You smoke like that in the Carpenter's Arms, my brothers'd
take you into the car park and kick your cunt in.
Leave you for dead.
I can blow smoke rings.
I'm trying to learn
To blow a smoke ring
In the shape of a (*Blows.*)
Cunt.

CASANOVA

For art ?

KAYLEIGH

For pleasure.

CASANOVA

Try again.

She blows again

CASANOVA

There. You've done it.

KAYLEIGH

No way.
You ever seen a cunt?
That ain't cunt. (*Blows.*)
These ones
Look mostly like
arseholes.
. . .
I feel sick now.

CASANOVA

Do you want a glass of water?

I'm gonna puke.
. . .
Stay there.
Don't fucking move.
I want you.
I'm gonna fucking have you.
I'll be back.

> *She exits.*
>> *Marie Louise beckons Casanova.*
>> *They exit.*

SIX

The Cabinet Maker's workshop.
  The Cabinet Maker is arranging flowers and
champagne on a cabinet
  He also sets up a little CD player with some music.

CABINET MAKER

Kate.
K.A.T.E.
Katie.
Kat.
Kitty.
Kath.
Kathy.
Katherine.
Kate.

SEVEN

Mrs Tennant and Marie Louise, in the gallery with the cases.

Mrs Tennant is examining the smoke-ring case.

MRS TENNANT

Kayleigh.
One thousand and four.

MARIE LOUISE

One thousand and five.

MRS TENNANT

Who else?

MARIE LOUISE

Me.

She shows her a broken 'No Smoking' sign from an aeroplane toilet.

MARIE LOUISE

On the aeroplane.
I went into the toilet.
He followed me in.
Shut the door, locked it.
He sat.
I sat on top of him.
I closed my eyes.
I held him.
We didn't move.
After an hour.
I didn't know any more
What was me, and what was him.
. . .
I have never ever felt so –
. . .

When the stewardess finally knocked on the door
And I opened my eyes
He was looking at me.
I had to turn my face away.
It's just where I'm from and what I'm made of.
Pleasure makes me feel ashamed.

MRS TENNANT

The sign is cracked. It's broken.

MARIE LOUISE

I hit my head on it when we stood up.

MRS TENNANT

I asked you not to fuck him.

MARIE LOUISE

I know.

MRS TENNANT

I thought you were stronger than that.

MARIE LOUISE

So did I.

MRS TENNANT

Why? Why did you . . . betray my trust?

MARIE LOUISE

He said – he thought – I was . . . the one.

MRS TENNANT

Lying bastard.

MARIE LOUISE

No, he wasn't lying.
He did think that.

MRS TENNANT

Where is he?

MARIE LOUISE

He's at the hotel.

MRS TENNANT

So. Are you the one?
Are you going to . . . to settle down with him?
Tame him?

MARIE LOUISE

He's not an animal.

MRS TENNANT

Answer the question.

MARIE LOUISE

No.
I'm not the one.
He was wrong.

MRS TENNANT

How do you know?

MARIE LOUISE

He told me.
It's someone else.
He realised as soon as we got off the plane.
As soon as he realised he was at home.

MRS TENNANT

Who?
Who is it?

MARIE LOUISE

You.
He's waiting for you.

MRS TENNANT

Marie Louise . . .

MARIE LOUISE

He's certain.

MRS TENNANT

Do you regret it?

MARIE LOUISE

No.
He opened a door.
I walked through.

MRS TENNANT

I owe you the wages for the month you worked.
And a month in advance.
And . . . take this as well.
As a thank you from me.
For your honesty. You could have lied.
The job's still open, if you want it.

MARIE LOUISE

I don't know – I don't know what I want to do.

MRS TENNANT

I'll need someone to help me organise the opening of the
gallery. Will you do that?
I can't do it on my own.

MARIE LOUISE

I'll help with the opening.
I'll work with him.
But then . . . I think maybe I'm going to disappear.

EIGHT

The Cabinet Maker arranges a bed.
He sets the music to play.
He arranges himself on the bed.
He decides the music is wrong.
He changes the music.
He arranges himself on the bed.
He wants to look natural.

Kate enters.
She is carrying a bottle of Bombay Gin.

KATE

I came back.

She takes in the scene.

CABINET MAKER

I was just . . . listening to some . . .

KATE

I came back to say – we can't do this.
We can't have confusion.

CABINET MAKER

I see.

KATE

I'm a professional. You hired me to do a job.

CABINET MAKER

Yes.

KATE

I can't mix . . . my work with . . .

CABINET MAKER

The job's cancelled.

KATE

Right.

CABINET MAKER

He's finished. Forgotten. An animal. That's all.
An animal, let him . . . go.

KATE

You're right. He's an animal.

CABINET MAKER

Less. He's a . . . I won't even say the word.
Don't even . . .
We won't mention him.

KATE

He . . . he.

CABINET MAKER

Shh.
You came back.
Stay,
Let me cook you a meal.
A curry . . .
I brought some wine.
And a video.
And I bought a camera.
I want to take a picture of you
To put in my wallet.
I bought a ring I want to give you.
I bought candles I want to put round your bath.
And oil to rub into your skin.
And chocolate.
And I washed the sheets.
And I fed the cat.
Stay.

KATE

Nice music.
I've never heard it before.

CABINET MAKER

You like it?

KATE

Did she like it?

CABINET MAKER

Yes.

KATE

Did it work for her?

CABINET MAKER

Yes.

KATE

I see myself in mirrors and I don't know who I am.

CABINET MAKER

I know who you are.

KATE

Do you?

CABINET MAKER

You're Kate.
You're my Kate.

Kate gets into bed with the Cabinet Maker.

NINE

Night.
Casanova on a hotel balcony.
Mrs Tennant enters.

MRS TENNANT

You brought the spring with you.
It's a warm night,
It's been cold as long as I can remember.

CASANOVA

The roof below, how far away do you think it is?

MRS TENNANT

A few yards.

CASANOVA

How high are we?

MRS TENNANT

Six floors.

CASANOVA

If your husband discovered us
Do you think I could still make the leap?

MRS TENNANT

Of course you could.

CASANOVA

I'm older than I was.

MRS TENNANT

So am I.

*A gunshot. Another gunshot. They don't duck, but
Casanova looks around in surprise.*

CASANOVA

What was that?

MRS TENNANT

Someone shooting a gun.

CASANOVA

Shouldn't we – throw ourselves to the floor?
Call the police . . .

MRS TENNANT

Don't worry.
It's normal these days.
The city's going to the dogs.

They bring in bags of tranquillisers
And distribute them from the back of lorries.
At night they drive through the city and shoot.
Just gunfire in the night.
It happens all the time.
They'll tell you it's a car backfiring, but it's some murder
or another. They clear up the bodies before dawn, and
cement them into the walls of luxury flats.
This used to be a city of knives.
At least a knifing requires that the victim and the killer
touch.
A hand against a stomach.
Now it's all guns and tranquillisers.

CASANOVA

The trouble with coming home
Is that you very quickly remember
All the reasons why you left.

MRS TENNANT

I own the city now. Most of it anyway.
You want some?
Have some.
There, the area by the water,
It's very fashionable now.
Take it.

CASANOVA

I only want that ledge, and the window opposite yours.
So I can spend the day watching you and the night with
you.

MRS TENNANT

Am I the same as I was?

CASANOVA

In every detail.

They kiss.

CASANOVA

You're the one.
You know that, don't you?
That's why I came back –

MRS TENNANT

I thought Marie Louise was the one.

CASANOVA

Look, I'm sorry about that . . .

MRS TENNANT

It's done. It doesn't matter.
What matters is that you came back.
The exhibition's ready.
You should see it.

CASANOVA

Fuck the exhibition.
I want you.

MRS TENNANT

You've had me.
You've had a thousand women.
This is your chance to fuck a country.

CASANOVA

They're all on tranquillisers.
I'll be fucking a corpse.

MRS TENNANT

So wake them up.
Show them life.

CASANOVA

I'm tired.
Catch a plane with me.
We'll go somewhere.
We'll live – leave them to rot.

MRS TENNANT

You have a thousand moments
That prove that there's more to life than death.
That you can steal life where you find it
And feel no guilt.
A thousand moments
that demand we squeeze every last possibility out of time –
That we defy fate.
That we piss against the wind.
A thousand rebellions against God.
And you want to keep them secret?

CASANOVA

It's enough. I've found what I want. You.

MRS TENNANT

Traitor.

CASANOVA

No.

MRS TENNANT

Liar.

CASANOVA

I'm telling the truth.

MRS TENNANT

I know you.
You seem to forget that.

CASANOVA

I know you too.

MRS TENNANT

All the time you were away, I dreamed of the day
You'd come back. I went to gallery openings and book
launches, first nights and loft apartment cocktail parties
and in every room I looked for you. I felt your shape in
everything I touched. Every time I closed my eyes to

sleep it was a picture of you I clung to –
Climbing down the drainpipe, standing half-dressed in
the dark on the roof of my father's double garage,
staring out across the starlit gardens of the village.
Knowing you existed, made it possible to be married.
Possible to be happy.
Because the idea of you was a door, I could unlock and
leave through.

CASANOVA

Leave your husband.
Take life . . . steal, just like you said.

MRS TENNANT

I like being married.
It's comfortable.

CASANOVA

Marry me.

MRS TENNANT

Don't be ridiculous.

CASANOVA

Cancel the exhibition.
It's all wrong . . . they were right after all . . .
We're made to be settled.
I can change.
I can find true happiness in the arms of one woman.

MRS TENNANT

You're just scared. It's only natural.

CASANOVA

We'll have a house in the suburbs.
And a lawn.
And a holiday cottage.
And we'll be kind.
And we'll give money to charities.
And car-share with the neighbours on the way in to work.

MRS TENNANT

You doubt yourself.
All artists doubt themselves.
The doubts prove your greatness.

CASANOVA

I can't face it alone.
I need you.
Stay with me. Fuck me. Be with me.

MRS TENNANT

I need you.
But I don't want you.

CASANOVA

How can you not want me?

MRS TENNANT

. . .

CASANOVA

You wanted me once.

MRS TENNANT

Your skin is grey.
Your eyes are hollow.
Physically you repulse me.
But this body isn't you –
You're the exhibition.
You're in the spaces between the cabinets.
I need –
This city needs – the possibility of you.
But to be with you?
No.
I'm not stupid.
I know what you're like.
That many women.
Marie Louise as well.
It's sick.
You have to admit it.

TEN

The Cabinet Maker in bed.
  Kate half-dressed, drinking Bombay Gin.

CABINET MAKER

I kept the cottage.
You could come to the cottage.
I haven't been back.
It's probably overgrown.
It has a barn.
I wanted to make the barn a workshop.
We could put a desk in.
You could have a desk in the barn.
We could –

KATE

What do you think he's doing now?
At this very moment?

CABINET MAKER

. . .
Kate.

KATE

What?

CABINET MAKER

I was talking about the cottage.

KATE

Doesn't it bother you that he's still –
Do I look like her?

CABINET MAKER

Yes.

KATE

I finally feel like I understand her.

CABINET MAKER

Good.

KATE

I feel like I know her.

CABINET MAKER

That's wonderful.

KATE

So I want to see him.
I want to finish it.
. . .
Where did she come from?
Your wife?

CABINET MAKER

Here.

KATE

So she spoke with my voice?

CABINET MAKER

Yes.

KATE

So what was her name?

CABINET MAKER

Her name . . .

KATE

It's just I noticed.
You never told me her name.

CABINET MAKER

He didn't know her name.

KATE

But you did.
Tell me.

CABINET MAKER

It's not important.

KATE

Tell me her fucking name
When I ask you.

CABINET MAKER

I can't.

KATE

I can.
Kate.
Her name was Kate.

Kate leaves.

ELEVEN

A sex club.
   The sound of applause.
   Casanova and Molly are at the bar.
   Molly has a tape recorder and is interviewing
Casanova.
   Casanova is drinking heavily.

CASANOVA

My idea of heaven is . . .

MOLLY

Can we go somewhere else?
I'm slightly uncomfortable with stripping.
I don't like this place.

CASANOVA

My idea of heaven is this place.

MOLLY

What song are they playing in heaven?

CASANOVA

This song.

MOLLY

What are you drinking in heaven?

CASANOVA

Gin.

MOLLY

Who's with you in heaven?

CASANOVA

You.
What's your idea of heaven?

MOLLY

Can we go somewhere else?
Maybe we could . . . talk.

CASANOVA

You know what I would like?

MOLLY

No.

CASANOVA

I'd very much like to rub some coke on my dick and
have you fuck me.
What do you say?

MOLLY

Do you want me to go into the box?

CASANOVA

Yes.

MOLLY

Do you want to see more?

CASANOVA

Yes.

MOLLY

Do you want me to open myself up so you can see right through me?

CASANOVA

Yes.

MOLLY

I can do that.
Put music on. I can move.
Wear cheap clothes. I can do that.
Do you want me to do that?
I can learn.
I can show you cuts on my arms.
Do you want me to do that?

CASANOVA

I want you to buy me another gin.

MOLLY

Here – have the bottle.

CASANOVA

Is it on expenses?
I don't want you out of pocket.

MOLLY

Come home with me.
Now.
We could have a curry.
Watch a video.
Have an ice cream and curl up on the sofa.
We could listen to music.
Or flick through the TV channels.
We could talk.

CASANOVA

You know you were asking me about heaven?

MOLLY

Yes.

CASANOVA

Well that – that you've just described to me –
Being truthful . . .
That
Is my idea of hell.
. . .
How far will the next one go do you think?
What will we get to see?
How long do we have to wait?

MOLLY

You need help.

CASANOVA

I need help to get some tranquillisers.
I want to buy some tranquillisers.
And maybe a gun.

Molly switches the tape recorder off.

MOLLY

Do you mind if I take your picture?

CASANOVA

Fire away.

Molly takes his picture.
The flash envelopes the whole stage.
She leaves.

TWELVE

The sex club.
  The Cabinet Maker is sitting beside Casanova.
  In the box, a woman is blowing smoke rings.

CABINET MAKER
I've been coming here for years.
Always sit in this seat.
Waiting for them to put something in that case,
That I recognise.
Never comes.
May as well be empty.
You enjoy the show?

CASANOVA
Not enough to satisfy.

CABINET MAKER
Enough to wait for the next act?

CASANOVA
Do you sell tranquillisers?

CABINET MAKER
Sometimes.

CASANOVA
You got any tonight?

CABINET MAKER
I've got anaesthetics.
Gas, injection, towel over the face.
You want some of that?
. . .
I've got sedatives.
Sleeping pills, beta blockers . . . whatever you want.

CASANOVA

You got tranquillisers?

CABINET MAKER

You know the helicopters,
That fly over the bush.
And the guy leans out with a gun.
Shoots a dart into the rhino.
Then they drag it into the back of a truck.
Take it to a zoo.
I've got some of that.

CASANOVA

I'll take some.

CABINET MAKER

Here.
Take that.
For the next twenty-four hours
You might as well be dead.

CASANOVA

Thank you.
I want a gun as well.

CABINET MAKER

I don't sell guns.

CASANOVA

I need a gun.

CABINET MAKER

Why?

CASANOVA

I think I may want to kill myself.

CABINET MAKER

I've run out of guns.
Everybody wants to kill themselves.

I can't keep up with demand.
If you want to kill yourself
Why don't you smash your head off a wall?
That's what everybody else does.
I've seen this act before.
It's no good.
Not what I'm looking for at all.
Take my seat.
You might enjoy it.

The Cabinet Maker leaves.
   In the case is the Boy Rock Star.
   He sings.
   After he sings he approaches Casanova's table.

BOY ROCK STAR

Do you know who I am?

CASANOVA

No.

BOY ROCK STAR

That's what I like about you. Everywhere I go in this city
I'm mobbed. They fucking love the shit out of me. And
it weighs me down, I'm telling you. I look ahead and all
I can see is more and more and more fame. I went to a
clairvoyant who works from an office above a pawnshop.
She told me she could see me amongst Amazonian Indians.
In a Yanomami village. I said, what – in another life?
She said – making a TV special. I like being with you
because you don't know me. Do you want to know the
artistic process I go through to make my music? Usually
a lyric comes to me first. You know, a line or a fragment
of a line – it's very mysterious – then I go into the studio
with the band and we throw ideas around – we just play
shit, you know, until we get a riff, and then we get it
down. Fast. And that's it. Rough as fuck. But that's how
I wrote all the big hits. All the ones they play in clothes

shops. I can't take the responsibility any more. The public are sucking the life-blood out of me. I read a magazine where one of my fans wrote: 'He seems such a straightforward fun-loving guy, The way he talked about his sadness over his estranged daughter – Jade – I felt a real connection with him.' I hold on to that. That's my touchstone. Do you want to come back to my flat?

THIRTEEN

Marie Louise in the Gallery.
She is checking the invitations.
Mrs Tennant enters.

MRS TENNANT
Have you seen the paper?

MARIE LOUISE
No.

MRS TENNANT
Some fucking bint of a reporter found him in a strip club.

MARIE LOUISE
Quelle surprise.

MRS TENNANT
He asked her for tranquillisers.
It's all on tape.

MARIE LOUISE
Did she fuck him?

MRS TENNANT
He turned her down.

MARIE LOUISE
Hell hath no fury.

MRS TENNANT

We'll need to put out a press release.
Who's coming?

MARIE LOUISE

All the politicians and their wives.
The art world.
The literary world.
The critics.
The main footballers.
Some of the criminals.
The music scene.
The important chefs.
The minority communities.
The funding bodies.

MRS TENNANT

They're all coming.
They'd have fallen at his feet.
And the bastard has to go and throw it away.

MARIE LOUISE

Do you want me to cancel the invitations?

MRS TENNANT

No.
For God's sake.
After what I've put into this.
No.
We carry on.
We just have to change the press release.

MARIE LOUISE

The ushers are coming in for the tour.
Do you want me to tell them anything?

MRS TENNANT

Tell them to keep their mouths shut and look pretty.
Lock up when you've finished.
I'll see you in the morning.

MARIE LOUISE

Goodnight.

MRS TENNANT

Oh, Marie Louise.
I knew I'd forget someone.
The Cabinet Makers.
Make sure to invite the Cabinet Makers.

MARIE LOUISE

We don't normally invite them.

MRS TENNANT

Even if nobody appreciates the contents, Marie Louise,
The Cabinet Makers will appreciate the cases.

FOURTEEN

*Casanova in the Boy Rock Star's flat. The Boy Rock Star
is boiling a kettle on a single gas ring.*

BOY ROCK STAR

I like to be punched.
I like to have boiling water poured on me.
I like to be hit with a belt.
I like to be burned with wax.
I like to be blindfolded.
I like to be cut.
I like to be hung.

CASANOVA

I can't do any of those things.

BOY ROCK STAR

Why not?
I invited you back to my fucking flat.
You don't know me.
What do you care?

CASANOVA

I can't hurt you.

BOY ROCK STAR

I have a knife.
I like to be stabbed.

CASANOVA

Why?

BOY ROCK STAR

What do you mean why?
It's what I like.

CASANOVA

But . . . pleasure.
Don't you like pleasure?

BOY ROCK STAR

Pleasure?
In this city?
Pleasure, in this city, is to be made to feel like shit.

CASANOVA

Look at me.

Boy Rock Star looks at Casanova.

BOY ROCK STAR

I don't like this.

CASANOVA

Don't speak.

BOY ROCK STAR

Don't.

Casanova approaches the Boy Rock Star and kisses him. Holds him. Touches him.

CASANOVA

This is pleasure.
I know you.
You're a star because you're beautiful.

BOY ROCK STAR

I am. I'm a big big star.

CASANOVA

They love you because they see
What I see.

BOY ROCK STAR

They love me.

CASANOVA

Because you're alive.

BOY ROCK STAR

I'm alive.

Casanova touches the Boy Rock Star between his legs.

CASANOVA

Who are you?

BOY ROCK STAR

I'm a boy.

CASANOVA

You're a woman?

BOY ROCK STAR

I'm a boy.
I'm a boy rock star.

Boy Rock Star breaks away.

BOY ROCK STAR

You'd better get the fuck out of my flat, mister.
I've got security here.

I've got my bodyguards just outside.
OK.
So go.

CASANOVA

If that's what you want.

BOY ROCK STAR

Sign this.

Scribbles a note on a piece of paper.

Fucking sign it.

CASANOVA

What is it?

BOY ROCK STAR

It's a fucking confidentiality agreement.
OK.
It's legally binding.
My lawyers had it drawn up.
You never tell.
You never breathe a word to the press.
Or I'll sue the shit out of you.

Casanova signs and leaves.

FIFTEEN

Marie Louise behind a desk, Kate sitting in front of her.

MARIE LOUISE

There are one thousand and six cabinets, each cabinet is named. Nothing is for sale. When we open the doors tomorrow, you will serve canapés and champagne. If anybody asks you anything, deny all knowledge. Sign this.

KATE

What is it?

MARIE LOUISE

It's a confidentiality agreement.
It's legally binding.

KATE

May I look around?

MARIE LOUISE

Of course.
Get the lie of the land.
It's important that everything works perfectly.

KATE

Have you met him?

MARIE LOUISE

Yes.
I've worked very closely with him.

KATE

What's he like?

MARIE LOUISE

Well, I have to be careful, I have signed the confidentiality agreement.
. . .

But . . .
He certainly lives up to his name.

KATE

Really?

MARIE LOUISE

Really.

KATE

Will he be there tomorrow?

MARIE LOUISE

He'll be there.

Kate exits.
Casanova enters.
He carries a bottle of Bombay Gin.

MARIE LOUISE

You.

CASANOVA

I wanted to look around.
Before the crowds.

MARIE LOUISE

You've got a cheek showing your face.

CASANOVA

I . . . coming home.
It's been more difficult than I thought.

MARIE LOUISE

I expected more from you.
Where did you go?

CASANOVA

I was . . . somewhere . . . I honestly don't remember.
It doesn't mean anything.
I promise.

125

MARIE LOUISE

You think you're fucking God's gift.
You're not.
You're lucky anyone takes pity on you.
You're a fucking mess.

CASANOVA

I just want to . . . sleep . . . with them. Again.

MARIE LOUISE

The light switch is on the left as you go in.

CASANOVA

Thank you.

MARIE LOUISE

I liked working for you.
I probably won't see you again.
After the opening, I'm going to disappear for a while.
I'm going to be a waitress in the desert.
I wrote to a roadhouse in Arizona.
They offered me a job.
. . .
I'll miss you.
. . .
You could come with me.
No.
Will you remember me?

CASANOVA

Every detail.

MARIE LOUISE

One thing,
Don't try and fuck the usher.
We've no time left to make another cabinet.

Marie Louise exits.
   Casanova enters the gallery.

SIXTEEN

In the gallery.
   Casanova looks around.
   He curls up on the floor.
   As if to go to sleep.
   In the semi-dark Kate appears.
   She goes to him.
   She starts to undo his fly.
   She makes as if to suck him off.

CASANOVA

Who are you?
. . .
Who are you?

KATE

Do you remember me?

CASANOVA

No.

KATE

Do you remember me?

CASANOVA

I don't remember you
But whoever you are, you're disguised as
The Cabinet Maker's wife.

KATE

You saw through me.

CASANOVA

I don't remember you,
But I remember her exactly.
Why have you got a gun?

KATE

The Cabinet Maker remembers.

CASANOVA

What are you talking about?
Are you on tranquillisers?
Are you going to kill me?

KATE

Say sorry.

CASANOVA

Why?

KATE

Say sorry to the Cabinet Maker.

CASANOVA

Is he here?
Why should I say sorry?

KATE

For the pain you've caused.
For . . .
Just do it.
Or else I have to kill you.

CASANOVA

How can I apologise, if I didn't do anything wrong?

KATE

You stole his wife.
Apologise.

CASANOVA

How can I steal a woman?
The Cabinet Maker's wife disappeared.
She became a waitress in the desert.

KATE

You took her away from him.

CASANOVA

I opened a door, she walked through it.

KATE

She was perfectly happy till you came along.

CASANOVA

When we fucked, she told me she thought of death.

KATE

You're a liar.

CASANOVA

I need a drink.
Do you want a drink?

KATE

. . .

He offers her the bottle.
She takes it.
She sits with him.

CASANOVA

She was happy.
I held her,
In the hotel bedroom.
In amber light.
The shape of her hips, the shape of her head.
She breathed easily.

KATE

She was sick.
You took advantage of her sickness.

CASANOVA

No.
He made her sick.

KATE

I love him.

CASANOVA

Then why aren't you with him?

KATE

He smothers me.

CASANOVA

Then leave him.

KATE

If I left him I'd spin away.
Without him I don't think I can hold on to reality.

CASANOVA

Then spin away.

KATE

You don't look like I expected.

CASANOVA

Life never does, when it happens to you.

KATE

Do I look like her?

CASANOVA

You look perfect.

KATE

This isn't right.

CASANOVA

We must find pleasure when we can.
And when we find it, take it.

KATE

Pleasure makes us forget ourselves.

CASANOVA

When we forget ourselves
We're suddenly alive.

KATE

He's waiting for me.

CASANOVA

Who are you?

KATE

I'm Kate.

CASANOVA

Who are you?

She breaks away from him.

KATE

Don't you understand?
You sick fuck.
I'm trying to save you.
I want to cure you.
You don't love yourself.
You're lonely.
You seek validation through sex.
You're an addict.
You've suffered abuse.
You repress.
You're incontinent.
You're a danger to the public.
You break up families.
You stop people wanting to work.
You give people ideas.
I want to cure you.
I have some tranquillisers.
Take them.

CASANOVA

I'm not sick.
The city is sick.
I'm still alive.

KATE

If you won't atone.
If you won't . . . stop.
Then you have to be contained.

CASANOVA

Do what you want.
I won't fight you.
But I will never apologise.

Kate leads him to the case. He enters. She shuts the case.

KATE

Desire is uncontrollable.
It is a destroyer.
He must be exhibited, as a warning.
It's better that the prison has no door
Than to let the prisoner touch the handle
And suffer dreams of escape.
Now we can see the sickness
And take pills to avoid the disease.
These are the rules of a good society.
Men must be fed.
Women must not disappear.
There are already enough waitresses in the American desert.
And too many badly nourished men.

SEVENTEEN

Lights up, the opening of the exhibition, Casanova on display.
The Cabinet Maker, Marie Louise, Kate, Mrs Tennant with champagne and canapés.

MRS TENNANT

To commit suicide,
And put oneself on display.
It's grotesque
I emptied all the other cabinets.
And left him there preserved.
Sallow and grey and irredeemably
Kitsch.
A monument to what every woman knows
That illicit sex
Is always more attractive in the fantasy
Than in the reality.

MARIE LOUISE

He's a warning to women,
Watch out for plausible men.
I know I was fooled.
But fortunately not for long.

KATE

He was ill.
Is so sad.
Awful really, I met him, he was interesting but –
It's a brilliant, brilliant exhibition
Because it tells us
To keep taking our pills.

CABINET MAKER

Looking at him
I realise,
Pleasure is a corrosive substance.

Fortunately, these cases, are strong enough to contain
uranium.
So as he rots,
We'll be able to witness his corruption
In total safety.

MRS TENNANT

It's the biggest event of the season.
This exhibition.
It's drawn record crowds.
Everyone's copying it.
Every other gallery's looking for a type of sickness
To put on display.
Honestly, this city.
If only they could generate their own ideas.

MARIE LOUISE

I met a lovely boy today.
A rock star.
He's spontaneous and lovable and kind and good with kids
and he only loves me.
I had a brush with danger,
I was considering a trip abroad.
But luckily I was saved
By true love
Which is hard work as a matter of fact.

KATE

We've bought a house.
The Cabinet Maker and me.
An old barn in the country.
And we're renovating it.
Creosoting fences, and clearing brush.
When it's finished
People can come and look at us living in it.

CABINET MAKER

My cases have been very well received by my peers.
They appreciate the detail,

The time and ingenuity that's gone into the construction.
But I say to them,
It's nothing really,
We all put the same effort
Into the house, the car, the wife, the kids.
Really every ordinary man is a hero,
And every ordinary woman a heroine.
Just – keeping going.
Just keeping our heads above water.
Until we die.

EIGHTEEN

A change.
  A sofa.
  A TV.
  A CD player.
  Kate flicking through an endless stream of foreign-language TV channels.
  The Cabinet Maker standing beside a glass bookcase with five books in it.

CABINET MAKER
I don't know how you can stand it that loud.
. . .
Do you mind if I turn it down?

  Using a remote, Kate mutes the TV. A CD is playing.

Why don't we switch it off?
Do you mind switching it off?
Do you mind?

  She switches the television off.

That's lovely music.
Very soothing.

We'll just sit here and talk and listen to music.

. . .

. . .

Have you left a radio on somewhere in the house?
I think you've left a radio on.
Do you mind?
The radio's blaring away in there.
I can hear it from here.
I can hear every word they're saying.

. . .

I don't know how you can hear yourself think.

. . .

Actually if you don't mind,
I'll just go through and switch it off.

> *He exits for a few minutes.*
> *She remains staring at the blank TV.*
> *She blows a smoke ring.*
> *He returns.*

I've switched it off.
Whatever programme it was, they were practically
hysterical.
Arguing.
Banging on.
So I switched it off.
Poured myself a nice glass of malt.

. . .

There was a rattle coming from somewhere in the
kitchen.
Do you ever notice the rattle?
I have noticed it. Sometimes.
I wondered if it was the fridge.
I had a look around.
Sometimes when two objects stand just a fraction too
close to each other they catch the underlying vibratory
hum of the fridge mechanism and they rattle.

I moved all the stuff in the fridge apart.
Yogurt pots, milk bottles, tins of beer.
To no effect.
I looked about more generally.
Sometimes it could be two objects yards away from the
actual fridge but still catching that underlying vibration.

. . .

It makes you wonder.
If there's apparent silence in the kitchen.
Are these hums somehow existing in the spaces in between
objects.
Waiting until the objects are close enough
For the hum to find expression.

. . .

I couldn't help but notice that we don't have much food in.

. . .

Do you mind if we turn it down a bit?
Just a little.

. . .

Actually that's too low.
I can hear the mechanism of the CD player scuffling
along.
Look.
Just switch the damn thing off.
If you don't mind.

. . .

You're very quiet tonight, darling.

. . .

I can't sleep at night for the noise of the owls in the barn.
We'll get a man in to poison them.

> *He sits next to her.*
> *She barely moves.*
> *He holds her.*
> *She does not move.*

> *The End.*